Managing Foreign Exchange Exposure

William Thomas

ISBN: 172067020X
ISBN-13: 978-1720670209

DISCLAIMER

The content presented in this book is intended for educational purposes. The author and publisher are not offering it as accounting, financial, or other professional services advice. While best efforts have been used in preparing this book, the author and publisher make no representations or warranties of any kind and assume no liabilities of any kind with respect to the accuracy or completeness of the contents and specifically disclaim any implied warranties of merchantability or fitness of use for a particular purpose. Neither the author nor the publisher shall be held liable or responsible to any person or entity with respect to any loss or incidental or consequential damages caused, or alleged to have been caused, directly or indirectly, by the information or programs contained herein. No warranty may be created or extended by sales representatives or written sales materials. Every company is different and the advice and strategies contained herein may not be suitable for your situation. Before You should seek the services of a competent professional before beginning any improvement program.

CONTENTS

WILLIAM THOMAS

PART I: INTRODUCTION

WILLIAM THOMAS

1 INTRODUCTION

On January 15, 2015, global financial markets faced unprecedented volatility. The Swiss National Bank announced the dismantling of its currency ceiling against the Euro. An exchange peg set at EUR/CHF 1.20 was abandoned. The Swiss implemented the peg during the financial crisis and had been in place since 2011. Given the 'safe haven' status of the Swiss Franc, the surprise central bank decision rocked currency markets. The announcement sent the Swiss Franc nearly thirty percent stronger against the Euro. EUR/CHF collapsed to levels reaching as low as 0.85.

The dramatic market movement was problematic for many reasons. For currency traders, liquidity evaporated. Many positions that were long Euros and short Swiss Francs were unable to unwind their positions. There was no availability to exit out of a losing position. Stop/loss orders were left unfilled as market makers were caught with a one-sided market. Banks faced significant losses and several foreign exchange brokers became insolvent.

For corporations with financial exposure to Switzerland, the sharp currency appreciation created a new dilemma for doing business. Companies importing goods from Switzerland faced significantly higher purchase costs. They could either cut margins or pass on the incremental cost to their customers. Swiss exporters became less competitive on price and had to decide between losing sales or cutting prices.

Surprise policy decisions such as the one from the Swiss National Bank are historically rare. In the aftermath of the Financial Crisis, increased foreign exchange volatility resulting from central bank activities has been on the rise. So-called 'currency wars' between nation-states have pushed overnight deposit rates into negative territory to stimulate inflation. Other unconventional easing methods have also been implemented to stimulate economic growth.

The increase in central bank activity creates new challenges for traders and corporations alike. Foreign exchange volatility has become more prevalent. Speculative traders who thrive on increased volatility can be left behind as traditional models for predicting directionality of currency movements fail to capture the increased influence of central bank stimulus programs on the economies. For corporations operating internationally, volatility can create financial risk to forecast and plan. Setting plan targets during the budget process increase in irrelevance and fewer companies seek to hedge their forecasted activities in fear of adverse impacts from market movements.

Companies must understand the foreign exchange market more than ever if they want to be competitive on a global scale. No longer are the days of pricing or purchasing in consolidated financials currency. Legacy methods to simplify accounting practices make companies uncompetitive in an increased global environment. Understanding foreign exchange means understanding the market, underlying mechanics of a doing business in another currency and also requires familiarity with hedging concepts and products to mitigate risks. Through comprehension of these principles, corporate treasuries and executive management can be better prepared for unforeseen events.

The Market

The foreign exchange marketplace offers immense liquidity, services the needs of individuals and corporations across the globe, and operates nearly every hour of the week. It is a global and decentralized market. It is the largest market in the world.

Each day over US $3.0 trillion in currency is traded. To put it into perspective, the average daily volume traded across all US equity markets approximately US $28 billion. It would take over a hundred trading days of equity volume to match the amount of money exchanged in a single day through the foreign exchange market. Billions of dollars in trades can be absorbed in seconds. The influence of a particular market participant in the marketplace can be nonexistent. Even central banks, who may interfere in the market at grand scale, can struggle to move the needle as they fight animal spirits to push their currency in the direction they wish to steer it.

Demand of one currency in relation to another determines the relative values for each currency at any point in time. Economic data and geopolitical news can ignite significant volatility within seconds of being announced. The sheer number of participants in economic and political events can lead to leaked information and positioning even before an event takes place.

Projections from expert forecasters on economic data influence changes in future exchange rates and can immediately impact exchange rates in the present. Positive economic data for an economy could cause a currency to appreciate dramatically in one situation. In another situation, a positive economic report could cause a selloff in the country's currency because it failed to reach market expectations or increase hawkish sentiment.

Participants

The foreign exchange marketplace contributes to the facilitation of global trade by providing access and liquidity to world currencies. Participants in the foreign exchange market are diverse and range from international banks, to central banks implementing policy, to corporate treasury managers hedging their exchange rate risk. Additionally there are several players in the industry which participate purely from a speculative perspective and seek to profit from exchange rate movements.

Intricacies of the market can be complex. The marketplace for foreign exchange can seem overwhelming or even confusing to many people who are not experienced in the industry. Rates are quoted in terms of one currency in exchange for another. Conventionally quoted prices can differ from the methodologies used in situations such as corporate planning.

Market forces span far beyond micro-level factors. Government intervention to adjust exchange rates to stimulate export trade demand may occur at any time, and has increasingly been a contributor towards market volatility. Volatility can ignite seemingly without notice as news flashes through the marketplace. By understanding core principles discussed in this book, readers can better plan and execute their foreign exchange activities more effectively.

Summary

Trading currency requires an understanding of a broad set of skillsets. Investing or trading in foreign currency, as with other types of investments, carries risk. The content within this book seeks to explain how the foreign exchange market functions and the fundamental aspects that are important to know when getting involved in the foreign exchange market.

The purpose of this book is to serve readers with an introduction to core concepts of the foreign exchange market. Although the principles covered in this book are applicable to a broad range of readers, primary emphasis is given to address businesses with international exposure. A reader working in a corporate treasury function would therefore find this content more useful than a speculative trader looking to take advantage of market movements. With international trade in mind, examples within the reading are covered from a transaction and hedging perspective.

Hedging a currency exposure can increase the overall exposure of a company if executed improperly. Given the risks associated with trading, it is important to consider aspects of an exposure prior to entering into any foreign exchange contract. Even with a risk management program, it can only be as effective as the forecasts and information used to implements it. A knowledgeable officer with a comprehension of foreign exchange, access to proper hedging tools, and full visibility into the exposure of a company can dramatically reduce the risk of error and contribute towards an effective hedging program.

Contents in the book begin with the most basic concepts of the foreign exchange market. The components and structure of a foreign exchange contract will initially be explained. Components and structure of a foreign exchange contract are the basic fundamentals of foreign exchange.

After reviewing the core principles of foreign exchange, the book dives into the concepts of risk management. Risk management is the method of taking an identified exposure and aligning the exposure with a hedging product to reduce the volatility risk associated with the exposure.

The next segment of the book will cover the practical aspect of foreign exchange. Using examples of different risk management products in real world situations, both the product and purpose should become more clear. Examples using spot contracts, forwards and more complex derivative products will be covered.

The last section of the book provides a brief insight to the

regulatory environment that exists in the foreign exchange market. The financial crisis of 2008 identified regulatory and compliance gaps in the marketplace. New and proposed regulatory measures have been created in order to reduce the likelihood of a similar crisis from reoccurring in the future. Although foreign exchange is mostly unregulated, there are regulation and policies that have developed which will change the way business in the industry is done for years to come.

2 HISTORY OF FOREIGN EXCHANGE

To understand the history of foreign exchange, one must also understand the history of money. Money in its current form today is a reflection of evolution of trading since the early days of civilization. Money is a means of exchanging one value from one person to another. While not always taking the form it has today, money evolved from a barter system to become one of the most complex concepts in trade.

Earliest human civilizations used livestock as storage of wealth. Animals were bartered for goods and services. Although bartering livestock was an effective means of trade, animals were not easily divisible, transferrable or storable. Bartering extended to other objects to address such issues. Shells, furs and other precious items were commonly used as a medium for goods and services.

The rise in metallurgy helped transform trade into the modern form of currency we have today. Metal coins were developed and used to trade for goods and services as early as the times of the Pharaoh. Coins were easier to transport and store in contrast to livestock and other objects. Coinage gained in popularity within kingdoms and society. Although more efficient than storing livestock, coins were still difficult to guard safely from theft.

During the times of the Roman Empire, Roman currency was based on the Augustan Currency System. A set-weighted silver piece, known as a denarius, was exchanged against gold coins or base metal fractional denominations. The denominations were collectively called aes and included metals such as gold, silver and copper. A denarius, for example, was intended to trade at one tenth the value of a gold piece. Just as in currency markets today, this exchange fluctuated throughout the history of the Empire as new factors contributed towards the perceived worth of one metal against the other. As one Emperor followed another, same did the images on the coinage. Coins were stamped with the face of the current Emperor.

Precious metal within coins did not hold constant over time. There were two forms of dilution used by Emperors in order to expand their purchasing power beyond their actual wealth. The first method was simply shrinking the size of newly minted coins. A smaller sized coin would require less precious metal to make but could be immediately noticeable to the eye. Another method known as 'washing' would cover a less valuable metal with a metal of higher value. A washed coin would appear to be whole. An Emperor could help expand his purchasing power in the short term to cover the cost of a war or large series of purchases. Both methods of expanding circulation are similar to printing of currency in the fiat system of today. Eventually the public becomes aware of diminished value of the newly minted coins and neighboring states would seek additional compensation to adjust for the devaluation of the coins traded.

Coins of higher metal value would disappeared from circulation over time. An arbitragers could take washed or otherwise diluted coins and exchange them for coins of higher value. Once obtained, higher value coins could be melted and transformed into diluted coins or simply held and stored.

Proliferation of the coinage system also meant opportunity for theft, misplacement. The need for a safe and reliable storage mechanism was sought. People looked to people and places they knew they could trust. Places of worship and private parties such as goldsmiths and silversmiths were the first parties to offer storage services. A fee was charged for storage service. Transportation and storage no longer became much of concern as these services provided relative safety for storage of wealth.

An early example of money transfer services took place during the Crusades. Orders of Knights developed systems for participants in the Crusades. The organization operated as a single entity and conducted business in multiple locations. Since Orders traveled under heavy fortification they operated as strong escorts at affordable rates. In one instance, Italian traders in 1249 in Cyprus remitted Syrian bezants to the equivalent in Paris. Notarial contracts as well as letters of credit have been well documented in this time.

Over the course of time, merchants began to issue receipts of deposit to their depositors. These notes represented the promissory of delivery of precious metal held in safe keeping. Notes were more easily exchanged than the underlying metal and were of equal value. Receipts of deposit eventually became an acceptable medium of money and paper began to be exchanged instead of transacting at the place of storage. The system of commodity money began to transform into a system of representative money. Although in circulation, coins were still commonly used mediums of exchange.

Societies developed their own monetary systems which added complexity between communities. A deposit receipt or coin in one community would not always translate into acceptable currency in another neighboring community. The discrepancy between communities created an arbitrage opportunity. Money exchangers, particularly in the Middle East, capitalized on the opportunity to exchange one currency for another. The earliest form of a foreign exchange market was created.

The need for storage and transfer of wealth created some of the earliest forms of our current monetary system. Coins and receipts of deposit transacted between parties to settle trade agreements. Differences in coins and types of deposits created the opportunity for the earliest forms of currency trading. The creation of representative money was a stepping stone into modern day foreign exchange.

Modern Day

"In the absence of the gold standard, there is no way to protect savings from confiscation through inflation [...] Deficit spending is simply a scheme for the "hidden" confiscation of wealth. Gold stands in the way of this insidious process. It stands as a protector of property rights."

- Alan Greenspan, Gold and Economic Freedom (1968)

Much of the development in foreign exchange has occurred in the last century. New financial instruments have been created as the needs of individuals, companies and nations has evolved. Global instability and trade resulting from the first world war gave rise to our modern day market.

Around the time of World War I speculation and foreign currency trading began to become prevalent. Governments did not look favorably of speculation in the markets as it created challenges for competing economies. After World War I the world experienced arguably the first currency war.

In the early 1930s the backdrop for the currency war was the Great Depression and possibly the Gold Standard. A fixing of a country's currency to the price of gold prevented too much money from being printed. Any printing of money would cause people to trade it in for gold. As economies such as the United States suffered during this period in time, policy-makers were limited in flexibility to deal with shocks to their economy.

On September 19, 1931, Britain took the sterling off of the Gold Standard. The result of the move led the sterling to depreciate against gold and the currency of gold-pegged countries. Norway and Sweden shortly followed Britain's path. Denmark later followed suite. Economies such as the United States were now at a disadvantage in global trade. The United States Congress passed the "Gold Reserve Act" in January of 1934. The act nationalized gold held by banks and monetized it by giving banks gold certificates that could be used as reserves at the Fed. In 1936 countries such as France and Germany abandoned the Gold standard.

At the end of World War II, the Bretton Woods Accord was passed. The agreement pegged major global currencies to the US dollar. The dollar was in turn pegged to gold at the rate of $35 per ounce. The accord allowed currencies to fluctuate by one percent from the standard. Although the accord did accomplish the goals of its charter, it ultimately failed.

In 1971 the Smithsonian Agreement was implemented as one more attempt to establish precepts of the Bretton Woods Agreement. Gold was reset to $38 per ounce as the official price. Europe and Japan faced revaluation of their currencies and the intervention bands were widened to 2.25% of the fix. By 1973 the gold-to-dollar peg was devalued again. Europe and Japan did not intervene in the market and free-floating currencies again prevailed. A free-floating currency is one which the exchange rate, or "price", of a currency is established by the buying and selling pressures in the open exchange marketplace.

Exchange rate stability was still desirable in Europe, particularly with the European Economic Community (EEC) currencies. The 'snake in the tunnel' was the first attempt at a European monetary cooperation. In 1972 the Basle agreement limited bilateral margins between one another's currency to 2.25%. The range implied a 4.5% maximum change between any two currencies in the group. When the US dollar became a free floating currency in 1973 the tunnel collapsed. In 1977 the plan all but collapsed and was left with a Deutsche Mark zone of currency. By 1978 the International Monetary Fund mandated "floating" foreign exchange rates.

Over two decades later Europe again sought currency stability. On January 1, 1999, the Eurozone nations introduced a unified currency, the Euro. The Euro officially replaced the legacy currencies of twelve nations. The initial members of the Euro included Austria, Belgium, Finland, France, Germany, Greece, Holland, Ireland, Italy, Luxembourg, Portugal and Spain. Today the currency is used by seventeen of the twenty seven member states of the European Union.

As part of the unified currency, the Eurozone nations follow a common monetary policy. Fiscal policy standards are maintained in order to keep member nations on a single track. Although each member nation continues to host its own central bank, all monetary policies are determined by the European Central Bank (ECB). The head of each nation's central bank serves on the governing board of the ECB.

The Value of Money

Leading up to 1973, paper money was often backed by precious metals held by governments. An issuance of money into the market would be backed by inventory of precious metals held by government. An owner of currency paper could theoretically trade in their currency for an equivalent piece of precious metal. This created confidence when a government issued new money into the market.

Currency today is not backed by precious metals and its relative value to precious metals and other currencies changes based on market forces. As history suggests in the previous section, managing precious metal reserves to currencies is difficult to manage in an international ecosystem.

Silver Certificates

In the United States, paper money issued between 1862 to 1971 were known as Legal Tender Notes. Silver certificates linked paper currency to silver, with denominations of $1, $5 and $10. A legal tender note

The image below shows a copy of a silver certificate issued in 1928.

Factors Backing Money

Without precious metal supporting the issuance of paper currency, what factors contribute to the valuation of such paper? Many countries like Switzerland still hold precious metal reserves. Almost all nations today hold reserves in currencies of other nations in contrast to only holding precious metals. It is important to understand that these reserves (precious metals or other holdings) are rarely a significant percentage of the money supply.

Three primary factors now back money:

1. The economic power of the nation.
2. The ability of the government to tax its citizens.
3. The stability and strength of the government issuing the money.

The value of a currency relative to other currencies will move when any of these three factors change. The direction of change between currencies is based on the net purchases and sales of a currency. Although this list contains the primary factors that back money, this list is not all encompassing. Other factors can also impact the exchange rate of a currency.

Foreign Exchange Today

The acceleration of international trade in the last century has helped shape today's foreign exchange market. Evolution of fiat currency, mixed with daily demand of currency from central banks and importers and exporters has created a unique and volatile ecosystem for currency trading. The relative value of one fiat currency to another requires assessing several different factors which in turn creates some uncertainty in the marketplace.

Exchange rate movements in the marketplace are based on the aggregate perception of currencies in relation to one another. Participants range for corporate treasurers hedging their international currency risk to market speculators looking to profit from market movement.

Money has come through a significant evolution over time. From bartering of goods to free floating paper currency, money has continued to progress to meet the needs of international trade. The past century has opened the door for new participants and products. The next chapters in the book will reflect on what drives the market as well as products used today to trade in the foreign exchange marketplace.

3 MARKET OVERVIEW

Today, the foreign exchange market is the largest market in the world. The market is a collection of participants connected through different mediums of communication with a purpose to purchase and sell one currency for another. Of the 193 United Nations member states, there are currently 182 current official or de facto currencies available.

Hedge funds, banks, brokerage houses, corporations and individuals all play a unique part in the market. There is no single current market rate. Rather than a single market price, currency exchange rates are derived from "interbank dealing" prices. The interbank exchange is a wholesale market. Interbank dealing is the top-level foreign exchange market where thousands of banks across the world exchange different currencies.

When transactions occur in the interbank market these rates are quoted and referenced as the current market rate for wholesale banking. Subscription services such as Bloomberg and Reuters provide indication rates based on the interbank dealing market and also help dealers and their clients with up to date news coverage on the market.

Where is the Trading Floor?

The foreign exchange market is a rather unregulated, decentralized marketplace. The results of decentralization is the absence of a physical trading floor as seen in other types of exchanges. Instead, transactions take place primarily through electronic transmission. A significant portion of trading activity is done between parties such as banks through the Electronic Broking Services (EBS). EBS is a wholesale electronic trading platform.

While there are other systems to access market liquidity, EBS accounts for a significant portion of daily flow. More recent liquidity provider services have appeared in the market. Market participants now have the ability to access pricing that is competitive to EBS without trading such platform. New technologies will most likely continue to cut into market share held by EBS.

The foreign exchange futures market is a dramatically different story. Futures contracts are traded at different brick and mortar locations around the world. There is the IMM in Chicago, SIMEX in Singapore and LIFFE in London. Futures contracts trade in standard size units of currency and tenors.

Financial Centers For FX

The foreign exchange market has no central location for transactions. Most traders are clustered in various finance centers around the world. The largest financial center in the world is London. New York City trails behind. The secondary tier of financial centers include Tokyo, Amsterdam, Paris, Zurich, Frankfurt and Singapore. There are also smaller sized trading centers throughout the world such as Toronto, Mexico City and Sydney. Smaller financial centers have less liquidity and therefore have less impact in the market.

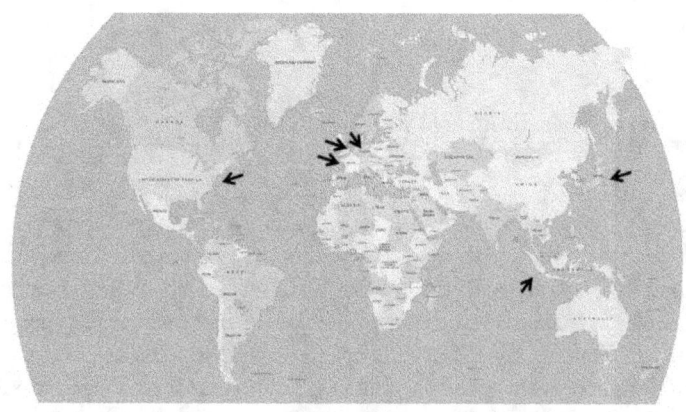

Trading of currency occurs almost 24 hours a day as markets open Monday morning in Australia and other finance centers come online as the day progresses across the globe. The market is most liquid during the typical trading ours of the major financial centers.

There are approximately fifteen most commonly traded currencies in the marketplace today. The most commonly traded currencies are often referred to as the 'Majors'. These currencies account for the majority of foreign exchange volume and are considered the most liquid.

The "Majors"

The Majors listed alphabetically:

AUD	GBP	NZD
CAD	HKD	SEK
CHF	JPY	TRY
DKK	MXN	USD
EUR	NOK	ZAR

Depending on the location of the trade, different currencies may be more prominent than other currencies for trade. For example, the global opening typically will have Australian Dollar and Japanese Yen as the highest volume currencies at that point in time.

Market liquidity often follows the timing of day in the local marketplace. Currency demand in one local market may differ than other markets. As business reaches end of day in a local market their currency may experience lower volume of trading. Often the best exchange rates occur during local time in the major trading hubs of the region.

4 TRANSACTION FUNDAMENTALS

An exchange occurs between two parties simply by exchanging one currency for another. The transaction can be done in the form of an outright or a swap. An outright is the most basic of trades where one party exchanges one currency for another. The exchange takes place for immediately delivery, called a spot transaction. If the exchange takes place in a future point in time the transaction is called a forward.

Two parties can also agree to exchange and re-exchange one currency for another. These types of transactions are called swaps. Examples of swap transactions will be discussed at a later point.

ISO Currency Codes

The International Organization for Standardization (ISO) has created a standardized currency coding system. Each currency is identified using three letters. The first two letters of the code represent the name of the country. The last letter denotes the currency name.

An example of this is the Japanese Yen, or JPY.

Code	Description
JP	Represents the identity code for Japan
Y	Represents the currency name, Yen.

Common Currencies:

ISO Code	Country	Currency Name
EUR	Europe (Region)	European Union Euro
JPY	Japan	Japanese Yen
GBP	Great Britain	English Pound (Sterling)
CHF	Switzerland	Swiss Franc
CAD	Canada	Canadian Dollar (Loonie)
AUD	Australia	Australian Dollar
NZD	New Zealand	New Zealand Dollar (Kiwi)

ISO codes are a simple means to communicate the currencies involved in a trade. If a party wishes to trade 'Pesos' with another party it would be difficult to discern if they are looking to deal in a currency such as the Columbian Peso, Mexican Peso, or even an Argentine Peso. The table below shows the dramatic difference between the three types of Pesos.

COP	1,781.91	Per USD
MXN	12.680	Per USD
ARS	5.0020	Per USD

Assume a USD 1,000,000.000 transaction was to be dealt in Peso. Not knowing the underlying could vary dramatically between the three currencies.

COP	1,781,910,000.00
MXN	12,680,000.00
ARS	5,002,000.00

The takeaway is the importance of clarity when dealing in foreign currencies to avoid making costly mistakes.

Foreign Exchange Contracts

A foreign exchange transaction must have a contract to outline the terms of trade. A foreign exchange contract is an obligation between two parties to exchange two different currencies at a specific rate on an identified date in time. Contracts are created to support the terms of trade.

Each party must show agreement of the exchange. To prevent confusion between parties, there are common components of a foreign exchange contract that need to be detailed. A contract can take the form of a written or verbal agreement.

Minimum Details of a Contract:

- The currency pair of the transaction and which currency is bought and which is sold.
- The exchange rate between the two currencies.
- The value (or settlement) date of the currency exchange.
- The trade (or contract) date when contract was arranged.
- The trading party name and addresses of the two parties in the contract.

Trading parties such as banks manage robust storage systems to document trades with counterparties. Tracking not only provides clients with details to aid in financial reporting, but banks require such detail to track its own positions and comply with regulatory requirements. Trading and sales desks commonly use recorded lines when communicating with clients. Recorded audio allows support for verbal agreements as a form of contract. Audio recordings are stored in archival in case there is a challenge to the outcome of the transaction upon question of either party in the deal.

Prior to the maturity of the contract both parties must provide settlement instructions for the contract. Settlement instructions provide both parties payment and receipt details of the funds. Proper and timely instruction sets are important to prevent delivery issues. Certain currencies, especially in developing economies, may require additional documentation or support for delivery.

Value Dates

The date at which a contract settles in foreign exchange is known as the value date. The most common designation for the value date is known as 'spot' which is defined as two business days (one day for Canadian dollar). "Forward" settlement is any day beyond spot and must be defined by a specific date.

Let's assume the trade date is November 4th.

Settlement	Value Date	Definition
Cash	November 4th	Same day settlement.
Value "tomorrow next"	November 5th	One business day settlement.
Spot	November 6th	Two business day settlement
Spot-next	Nov 7th	One day beyond Spot
Forward outright	Nov 7th or later	Three or more business day settlement

Market exchange rates are quoted at "Spot" settlement. Settlement can occur earlier or later than spot and must be defined at the time of the transaction. If a trading party does not identify the value date at the time of the transaction it will be quoted at "Spot." Two day settlement is standard because it provides both trading parties enough time to arrange for delivery. Transactions that settle sooner than spot must take into consideration time zone differences (local time) of both parties. Depending on the time of day of each trading partner you may be unable to process settlements for "cash" value.

Settlement occurs on standard business days. In cases where the value date lands on a holiday the settlement moves to the next available business day. For instance, if a bank holiday lands on November 6, a spot transaction would settle spot on November 7. If November 7 is a weekend, then the spot value date would be the following Monday.

Although Spot settlement is typically two business days, settlement between the United States and Canada (USD/CAD) is only one business day. If settlement of a trade is different than spot there may be an adjustment in the rate based on interest rate differences in the currency countries. A delivery beyond spot is called a 'forward' transaction and will be discussed later.

Exchange Rate Quotation Terms

There are two currencies that are exchanged in a contract. One party is buying currency A and selling currency B while the second party is selling currency A and buying currency B. When an exchange rate is shown it is important for each party to understand which currency is quoted in terms of the other.

Example:

The New Zealand Dollar exchange rate today is 0.8207.

Does that mean it is 0.8207 New Zealand Dollars for 1 US Dollar? This quote could also be quoted to mean 0.8207 US Dollars per New Zealand Dollar. Maybe the US Dollar is not even part of the exchange rate. Without knowing the currency pair quoted and terms of the quote for unit of one currency for another currency, it is difficult to determine what a market quote means.

There are standard market conventions for exchange rate quotes. Standardization helps both sides of a transaction easily determine the market rate without causing confusion.

Exchange rates are quoted in different methods. They can be quoted as either "direct" compared to "indirect" terms. Quotes can also be known to be reflected in "American" compared to "European" terms. Depending on the quoting convention, the rate may need to be inverted to match your particular reporting needs.

The important takeaway is that it is essential for each party to understand the quotation format before entering a contract. Communication is important when entering into a foreign exchange contract as the outcome can be differ greatly from expectations if not done correctly.

"Direct" vs. "Indirect"

Depending on quotation terms, calculating the amount of one currency for another would be conducted by either multiplying or dividing the currency you wish to exchange. Exchange rates can be quoted either in 'direct' or 'indirect terms which dictates the mathematical calculation of currency needed of one currency for another.

Direct Terms:

Exchange rate quote is based on the number of units of your local currency needed in exchange for one unit of foreign currency.

Indirect Terms:

Exchange rate quote is based on the number of units of a foreign currency needed in exchange for one unit of your local currency.

To determine the amount of currency you need to know whether the currency pair is quoted in direct or indirect terms. Depending on the quotation terms for a contract you would multiply or divide the currency by the exchange rate.

$$\frac{1}{Direct} = Indirect \qquad \frac{1}{Indirect} = Direct$$

American vs. European Terms

Similarly to the direct versus indirect quoting style, the quotation terms can also be considered in either American or European terms. Both terms detail how a currency rate is quoted and can be used interchangeably. Currencies such as the Euro, British Pound, and Australian Dollar are all quoted in American terms. Other currencies are often quoted in European terms.

Definition:

American terms: Currencies which are quoted in the number of units of US dollars per one unit of another currency are considered quoted in American terms. An example of a currency quoted in American terms is British Sterling (GBP) which typical market convention quotes as GBP/USD.

European terms: A currency that is quoted in the number of units of foreign currency per one US dollar is considered quoted in European terms. An example of a currency quoted in European terms is the Mexican Peso (MXN) which is quoted as USD/MXN.

$$\frac{1}{European} = American \qquad \frac{1}{American} = European$$

$$\frac{1}{MXN\ 13.2500} = USD\ .0755 \qquad \frac{1}{USD\ .0755} = MXN\ 13.2500$$

Bids and Offers

Standard market quotes for currency are given in pairs. On the left side you are given a bid, on the right side you are given an offer. Market makers give you a different rate depending on whether you are buying or selling an underlying currency (typically US Dollar).

Which side of the market are you? The market maker will always buy the base currency on the bid and sell the base currency on the offer.

Bid – On the bid the market maker will buy the base currency in exchange for the pair currency on the left hand side.

Offer – On the offer the market maker will sell the base currency in exchange for the pair currency on the right hand side.

The difference between the bid and offer is known as the bid-offer spread. This is the profit the market maker takes for creating a two way market.

Before executing a trade it is important to know which currency is to be purchased and which currency is to be sold. There are standard market conventions which specify the pairing order of currencies so it is important to know which side of the exchange you are on to avoid 'doubling up' on a position. As a guideline, the market maker will quote in terms of the base currency.

Bids and Offers in American vs. European Terms

The bid and offer quoted for a currency depends on which currency is the base. If the quote is provided in American terms, the bank's bid and offer is for the foreign currency. However, if the quote is provided in European terms, then the bank's bid and offer is for US dollars. To lean on the safe side it helps to communicate which currency you too to buy and which currency you wish to sell.

The example below reflects the exchange rate between the British Pound and US dollar. The example includes a "bid" and "offer" quotation for both sides of the market. The difference between the buying and selling price is known as the "spread."

Market Rates

American		European	
Bid	Offer	Bid	Offer
0.6208	0.6207	1.6107	1.6111

In American terms for the example above, 0.6207 is the offer for British Pounds and 1.6111 is the offer in European terms for US dollars. One could mistakenly believe they are receiving an erroneous rate if they misunderstand the quoting convention. Another way to say this is that a rate of 1.6111 indicates a bank would sell British Pounds in exchange for US dollars at the ratio of 1.6111 US dollars for each British Pound. The exchange rate shows the ratio of one currency per unit of another. The quotation in American terms is a bid and offer for British Pounds in relation to US dollars. The quote in European terms is the bid and offer for US dollars in relation to British Pounds.

If you have British Pounds and you contact the bank for a quote, the bank would give you a bid rate of 1.6107 in European terms or 0.6208 in American terms.

If you have US Dollars and you contact the bank for a quote, the bank would give you an offer rate of 1.6111 in European terms or 0.6207 in American terms.

Bids / Offers Chart:

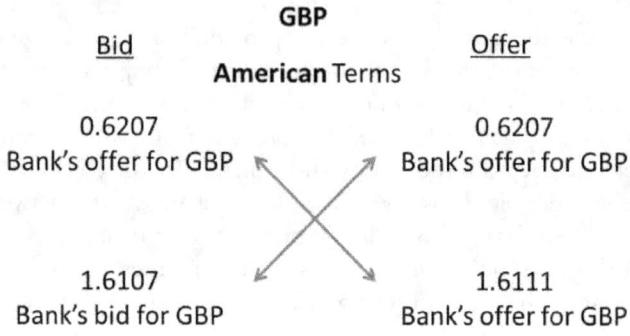

GBP

Bid   Offer

American Terms

0.6207   0.6207
Bank's offer for GBP   Bank's offer for GBP

1.6107   1.6111
Bank's bid for GBP   Bank's offer for GBP

European Terms

Notice how the exchange rate between European and American terms are the exact inverse of one another. Multiplying or dividing a foreign exchange rate can yield a different result. If an organization prefers the exchange rate to be quoted in one method or another they can request which term they prefer from their counterparty. Corporate systems can often be designed in the company's local currency making it difficult for certain operational functions to easily enter the appropriate rate into their financial system.

> Example:
> Client buys GBP 1,000,000.00 from the bank.
> Dealer Quote: GBP / USD 1.6107

GBP 1,000,000.00   X   1.6107   =   USD 1,610,700.00

USD 1,610,700.00   X   0.6208   =   GBP 1,000,000.00

Depending on the quotation terms of the trade, either reporting method will result in the same outcome. Each currency pair has a standard market convention, however identifying your preference in quotation terms before initiating the trade can provide clarity to both sites of the transaction.

Cross Rates

Exchange rates are often quoted with the US dollar (USD) quoted as part of the pair. There are times when the USD is not part of the currency pair. When an exchange rate is quoted in terms of one foreign currency for another foreign currency, this is known as a cross rate.

General Guidelines For Cross Rates:

The first thing to consider when dealing with cross rates is the underlying currency terms. There are two different considerations to help guide you in determining the correct pairing of currencies.

If two currency pairs are quoted in American terms:

Divide one exchange rate by the other. Generally this is the larger number divided by the smaller number. Some currencies trade near parity so close inspection is needed to make sure the right algebra is used.

Example for American Terms

EUR/USD = 1.3220

GBP/USD = 1.6120

To determine the EUR/GBP cross rate, divide the EUR/USD exchange rate by GBP/USD quote:

1.3220 / 1.6120 = .8201 British Pounds per Euro

If two currencies are quoted in European terms:

Follow the same process used above for American terms.

Example for European terms

USD/MXN = 12.7000

USD/CAD = 1.0010

To determine the CAD/MXN cross rate, divide the USD/ MXN exchange rate by USD/CAD quote:

12.7000 / 1.0010 = 12.6873 Mexican Pesos per Canadian Dollar

If one currency is quoted in European terms and one is quoted in American terms:

Multiply the two rates together. The rate derived will reflect the units of the lower value currency per one unit of the higher value currency.

Example for European and American Terms

USD / CHF = .9130

EUR / USD = 1.3237

Then the EUR/CHF cross rate would be the product of USD/CHF rate and EUR/USD.

0.9130 X 1.3237 = 1.2085 Swiss Francs per Euro

Forwards

As discussed in the settlement section, a "forward" transaction is defined as an exchange that takes place beyond spot value. This means that a transaction is to settle three days or beyond, with the exception of Canada, is considered a forward transaction. All major currencies as well as most other currencies have a forward market. Currencies such as the Euro, British pound, Japanese yen and Swiss franc can be traded several years forward. Other less traded currencies can be limited to less than a year.

A forward transaction comprises of two parts – a spot price and forward points. The spot part of the forward is the current market rate as if you were to settle within the normal spot range, for example two days. In addition to the spot component there are forward points. Forward points are calculated based on the differential in the interest rate between the two currency countries. The interest rate component can be at a premium or discount to the spot rate depending on the interest rate effect. The forward points compensate for holding a particular currency until delivery.

Forward Premiums vs. Discounts

The interest rate differential between the two currency countries determines the forward point adjustment for a forward exchange transaction. These points make an adjustment to spot at either a premium or a discount.

> Forward Premium: If the all-in price of the exchange rate is greater than the current spot it is said to trade at a forward premium.

> Forward Discount: If the all-in price of the exchange rate is less than the current spot exchange rate it is said to trade at a forward discount.

The difference between the current spot and forward price is called the forward premium or discount. The value of the adjustment is stated in "forward points", or simply "points". These forward points are added to, or subtracted from, the spot rate to determine the all-in forward rate. A "point", or "pip", is defined as the last decimal place to which a currency exchange rate is standardly quoted.

American Terms:

The example below shows how forward points impact the rate of exchange is the Euro against US dollar.

Market Rates

Spot EUR / USD:	$ 1.3220
1 Month Forward:	$ 1.3232
6 Month Forward:	$ 1.3253
1 Year Forward:	$ 1.3280

Notice how the exchange rate of the forward increases from spot out to one year. The rate of exchange is increasing so the Euro is considered to be trading at a forward premium to the US dollar. To calculate the forward premium, simply subtract the spot rate from the forward rate.

European Terms:

Currencies quoted in European terms differ in premium and discount compared to currencies quoted in American terms. Remember that currencies reported in European terms are reported in the number of foreign currency units for one US dollar.

Market Rates

Spot USD / CHF:	CHF 0.9132
1 Month Forward:	CHF 0.9128
6 Month Forward:	CHF 0.9102
1 Year Forward:	CHF 0.9068

The price for the US dollar in terms of Swiss francs is lower for each of the forward delivery dates. In this example the U.S. dollar is considered trade at a discount to the Swiss franc. Conversely, the Swiss franc is said to trade at a forward premium to the US dollar.

General Guidance:

Use the simple math equation with the table below to guide you.

$$Forward - Spot = A$$

	If A is positive...	If A is negative...
American Terms	Premium	Discount
European Terms	Discount	Premium

Forward Trade Bids and Offers

The forward market is quoted similar to the spot market and it has a two sided price. There is a bid and offer for the spot component as well as a bid and offer for the forward rate component. Forward quotes are normally quoted only in terms of forward points.

Here is an example taken of Swiss francs taken from a typical platform screen.

Market Rates:

	Bid	Offer
Spot CHF	0.9129	0.9132
1 Month	- 6.00	- 4.00
All-In	0.9123	0.9128

Remember, if the offer side of the forward points is greater than the bid side, the forward bid and offer are premiums and should be added to the spot bid and offer. Conversely, if the offer side of the forward points is smaller than the bid side (and both the bid and offer are positive numbers), the forward bid and offer are discounts and should be subtracted from the spot rate.

The example above shows the US dollar at a discount to the Swiss franc. The Swiss franc is at a premium to the US dollar based on a one month period.

Swaps

A foreign exchange swap is a simultaneous purchase and sale of identical amounts of one currency for another currency with two difference value dates. Corporate clients often use swaps to fund their foreign exchange balances.

Uses:

- Hedge for currency borrowings or investments.

- Maintain a currency position while gaining the use of a second currency for a period of time.

- Alter the delivery date of a previously negotiated forward contract.

A typical swap would include a spot transaction and a forward component. The purchase and sale are each considered "legs" of the deal. The closest transaction is called the "near leg" of the deal and the future offsetting transaction is called the "far leg" of the transaction. The near leg can sometimes be further in time than a spot deal. In this case it would be called a forward-forward swap. If the near leg is a point in time in the future then forward points may be adjusted for timing.

The price of a swap consists of both a spot and forward rate component similar to a regular forward. In a swap transaction the spot price is the same for both the near and far leg of the transaction even though one is a purchase and the other is a sale. The forward points of a swap reflect the difference in interest rates between the near and far leg of the deal.

Forward points in a swap transaction are determined by the far date of the transaction.

Example:

Company A enters into a one-month GBP swap against USD where they sell GBP at spot and buy the GBP back in one month.

Market Rates:

	Bid	Offer
Spot GBP	1.6153	1.6157
1 Month	- 3.00	- 1.00

Company A would sell their GBP at a spot rate of 1.6153, which is where the bank buys GBP. On the far leg of the position Company A buys back the GBP at the rate of 1.6152 (1.6153 plus the forward discount of -1 points). If the company were to do two separate transactions they would have sold their GBP at a spot of 1.6153 and they entered into a one-month forward contract at the rate of 1.6156. The company would have given up 3 additional points on the forward if they entered into two separate contracts.

PART II: RISK MANAGEMENT

5 FOREIGN EXCHANGE MOVEMENT

Currencies trade almost every hour of the day. Movement in exchange rates can happen without notice as news of events flash across various communication channels. Time of trading and volume can lead to significant volatility.

Exchange rates move in relation to other currencies due to many different factors. Throughout history we have seen how balance of payments, inflation, capital flows and the rate of growth have provided common themes in the market. It is important to understand how long term economic fundamentals comingle with short term factors that are psychological and technical.

Causes of Exchange Rate Movement

Exchange rates move in relation to other currencies due to many different factors. Throughout history we have seen how balance of payments, inflation, capital flows and the rate of growth have provided common themes in the market. It is important to understand how long term economic fundamentals comingle with short term factors that are psychological and technical.

Purchasing Power Parity

Recall that most currencies are free floating in the market. While central banks hold some amount of assets, currency fluctuations relative to other currencies is not based on tangible assets. Instead foreign exchange rates are based on the aggregate supply and demand of one currency in relation to another currency. Purchasing power parity (PPP) is an economic theory that is used to determine the relative value of currencies. This "law of one price" does not account for transaction costs or trade barriers. By comparing the price of a standard "basket of goods" in different countries you can determine the relative value of currencies.

Example:

The current GBP / USD exchange rate is 1.6120.

One Gallon of Milk (USD):	3.50
	÷
GBP / USD Exchange Rate:	1.6120
PPP Implied Cost of Milk (GBP):	2.17

PPP would suggest that cost of milk in GBP would be proportional to the weakness in US Dollar compared to the British Pound. If the price is actually GBP 3.50 in Britain, one could earn arbitrage profits by purchasing a gallon of milk in the US and selling it in Britain for a profit. Demand would increase in the US for milk driving up prices. Supply would increase in Britain and cause prices to decrease. The arbitrage changes to supply and demand would create a new equilibrium.

The Economist, a well-known weekly news and international affairs publication, popularized the Big Mac Index. The index compares the price of a Big Mac burger in McDonald's restaurants across different countries. The law of one price is tested by the Big Mac Index as the input costs differ substantially between countries. Positioning in the market also tests this theory since some emerging countries represent McDonald's as an expensive niche product. Even with potential flaws, the Big Mac Index is one of the best measures of purchasing power parity available.

Balance of Payments

The accounting record of all monetary transactions between a country and the rest of the world is known as balance of payments (BoP). Exports and imports of goods, services, financial capital and financial transfers are all transactions included in this calculation. The reported amount is prepared in a single currency which is generally the currency of the country concerned. Balance of payment is a useful benchmark in forecasting short-term market potential. A deficit in the balance of payments may create an excess supply of that country's currency in the marketplace. Conversely balance of payments surplus may lead to an increase in import purchases.

The balance of payment comprises of two principal parts – the current account and the capital account.

Current Account

The current account is a measure of balance of trade. More simply put, the current account reflects the net income of a nation. It is the sum of net revenue on exports minus payments for imports, factor income (net earnings on foreign investment) and cash transfers. A surplus in the current account means that a country is earning more on foreign trade than it is spending. Conversely, a deficit in the current account shows the country is spending more than it is earning and creates excess demand for foreign currency. This excess demand for foreign currency lowers the country's exchange rate until pricing equilibrium returns.

Current Account Breakdown

+	Net Exports (Exports – Imports)
+	Net Income Abroad
+	Net Current Transfers
=	**Current Account**

43

Capital Account

The capital account, or financial account, is a measure of the net change in ownership of foreign assets. It reflects the flow of national ownership of assets. If there is a capital surplus, it means that money is flowing into the country. Conversely if there is a capital deficit it means money is flowing out of the country, but also suggests that the nation is building foreign assets.

Capital Account Breakdown

	Foreign direct investment (FDI)
+	Portfolio investments
+	Other investments
+	Reserve account
=	**Capital Account**

Putting It Together: Balance of Payments

The balance of payments is the combination of the current account, capital account and adjustments for errors. The total balance of payments can be calculated with the formula below.

Balance of Payments Composition

	Current Account
+	Capital Account
+	Short Term Capital
+	Error and Omissions
=	**Balance of Payments**

It is important to remember that the balance of payments is a system of account of economic transactions between a country and its trading partners. Economists and market participants assess net flow between countries to forecast currency movements. Although balance of payments is a valuable data point, there are other factors that influence foreign exchange movement.

Other Causes of Exchange Rate Movement

Purchasing Power Parity and Balance of Payments are two important measurements when looking at foreign exchange movement. They are not the end-all, be-all of foreign exchange. Many factors in an economy or global environment can sway exchange rates between currencies. Some important factors are below but are not all encompassing.

Inflation

The rate at which the general level of prices for goods and services rises is known as inflation. A heating economy has an increase in demand for products which leads to higher prices for those products. This increase in prices creates diminishing purchase power of a currency. The differential in inflation rates between countries can signal how a currency will move in relation to other currencies. A higher inflation country will see its currency weaken against other currencies.

Interest Rates

The rate paid by a borrower for the use of money from a lender is known as the interest rate. Interest rates can create a change in the demand and supply of money. For example, if the interest rate in Britain in 3% and the interest rate in the US is 1%, investors would earn a higher return on their money by moving their money into British debt. Similar to inflation rates, the differential in rates between currency countries creates foreign exchange rate movement. The change in supply and demand for a currency based in changes in interest rates is known as interest rate parity.

Interest Rate Parity

Interest rate parity suggests that investors are indifferent among available interest rates in two countries. This is because foreign exchange rates between two countries are expected to adjust such that the return on a domestic deposit is equal to the foreign deposit return.

$$(1 + i_d) = \frac{E_t \, (S_{t+n}) \, (1 + i_f)}{S_t}$$

Where:

- $E_t \, (S_{t+n})$ is the expected future spot exchange rate at time t+n
- S_t is the current exchange rate
- i_d is the interest rate in the domestic country
- i_f the interest rate in the foreign currency country

There future foreign exchange rate offsets an arbitrage opportunity between different interest rates. Although this theory may not be perfect, it is a fundamental theory used in calculating forward exchange rates in the marketplace. We will review forwards at a later time.

Current Events

Monetary and fiscal policy both can create market movements. There are other short term factors to consider that can jolt exchange rates. Market psychology plays an important role in the day to day movements of exchange rates. If the political environment were to change, become more disjointed. Uncertainty around upcoming elections or legislation can cause markets to fluctuate. Natural disasters such as floods can disrupt economies and create pressure on currency markets as a result. Technical analysis is used to read market psychology to try to predict where the markets may move irrespective of market events.

6 RISK MANAGEMENT BASICS

Previous chapters defined different types of exposures inherent in conducting international business and what impacts foreign exchange markets. Corporate treasury must take additional measures to identify inherent internal risks to their company and implement risk management solutions to mitigate adverse foreign exchange market movements. Internal risks can be specific to company and may not translate equally across other parties.

Sources of Foreign Exchange Risk

Foreign exchange risks can have both economic and accounting impacts on a business. Broadly speaking, the underlying risk factors can be deduced into four common sources.

Cash Flow
Balance Sheet
Translation
Remeasurement

Considerations Before Hedging

A successful hedging program can be expensive to implement and manage. If done improperly a hedge can create significant risk to a company. Whether or not a company should hedge is company-specific based on their needs. Many companies decide not to hedge altogether. It may or may not be the most risk-adverse approach. Remember, the benefit of a hedging program should always outweigh the risks of exposure and the cost to manage such risks.

It is recommended to seek input from several different sources before deciding whether hedging is the right decision for your company. Accountants, economists, foreign exchange dealers, economists and your corporate treasury team are all great resources to speak to. Since every business is different there is no standardized approach.

Importance of Data

The foreign exchange specialist within a company receives information from accounting, budgeting, tax and treasury. Each provider of information has a unique perspective on the business and foreign exchange needs. As a foreign exchange specialist, data collection and analysis can be a daunting task. Many companies rely on enterprise resource planning (ERP) systems to identify net currency exposures. However, not all companies have such a system. One advantage to an ERP system is the ability to easily identify booked exposures.

Accounting for Subsidiaries

Tracking the change in cash flow can assist the foreign exchange specialist in aggregating foreign exchange needs by currency. As part of a hedging policy, the change in cash flow can be hedged through foreign exchange contracts. Different methodologies for tracking cash exist depending on the structure of data available to the foreign exchange specialist. The example below shows tracking of cash based on a common currency.

Example:

	Jan	Feb	Mar	Apr	May	Jun
Forecast	£5,100	£5,000	£5,200	£5,500	£5,250	£5,300
Actual	5,125	5,200	5,250	5,350	5,400	5,350
Variance	25	200	50	-150	150	50
% Variance	4.9%	4%	9.6%	-2.7%	2.9%	0.9%

Variances in actual cash positions compared to forecast should be monitored. Depending on policy such variances may require additional hedging.

Foreign Currency Accounts

Companies which have recurring operations in a foreign currency may benefit by opening a foreign currency account (FCA) in the respective currency country. A foreign currency account is a transactional account denominated in a currency other than the home currency. The FCA is maintained by a bank either in the home country or another country.

An advantage of a foreign currency account is the ability to hold excess cash without the need to convert back to the functional currency of the company. This could potentially save the company money through minimal currency conversions. Most banks, however, charge fees for managing an FCA account so it is important to assess the cost and benefit of managing such account.

Netting Agreements

One advantage of an FCA account is its ability to reduce the volume foreign currency conversions. If a company makes and receives payments in the same currency then multiple transactions can be netted against each other. Netting of payment and receipts leaves only a net difference to be monitored from a hedging perspective. This can also be done when different entities have foreign exchange payments between each other. An approach to limit foreign exchange conversions in such instance is known as a netting agreement.

There are three common different approaches to netting:

- **Unilateral netting agreement:** Aggregates cash flow among different subsidiaries. The company determines if any foreign exchange payments between subsidiaries can be netted. Only the residual balance is shifted.

- **Bilateral netting agreement:** Two companies in different countries conduct business with each other. The companies track payments owed to each other and then net out the balance at the end of the month. Only one party pays the other based on the net amount owed.

- **Multilateral netting agreement:** Multiple companies in different countries conduct business with each other. The complexity of such operation requires a centralized netting system. The payments are tracked in a centralized database and creates a net position for each participant to settle.

Netting agreements are typically contractual agreements. There are some countries which do not recognize the ability to enforce a netting agreement. The reasoning being such contract can undermine the rights of third-party creditors. Although there are risks associated with netting agreements, if done correctly, they can be a highly effective way to reduce foreign exchange transaction costs.

7 SEVEN STEPS TO RISK MANAGEMENT

There are several methods used to cover an exposure through hedging. Each solution has its own benefits and drawbacks. Regardless of the different hedging approach, every risk management program requires a framework to guide participants in the program.

The process to developing a foreign exchange management program can be simplified into seven categories:

Step	Description
1.	Define Objectives
2.	Qualify Exposures
3.	Quantify Exposures
4.	Develop Risk Management Strategy
5.	Implement Strategy
6.	Monitor Exposures & Hedges
7.	Review Performance

Define Objectives

A company should define its corporate risk management policy. In its framework it should identify the objectives of the risk management program and determine to what degree the company is willing to accept certain risks. Each risk may impose a varying degree of exposure to the company and the cost to manage such risk may exceed the benefit of mitigation. For risks where the company does not have a competitive advantage it may be beneficial to offset the risk. Foreign exchange is often an area where a company seeks to offset its risk.

Objective Considerations:

The amount of risk the company is prepared to accept can be defined by limits such as:

- By country
- By currency
- By value (size)
- By timeframe

Every business has its own risk tolerance and points of focus from a risk management perspective. There is no one right objective when considering risk management. Each company may have their own objective considerations which may span outside of the four dimensions we have mentioned.

Qualify Exposures

As discussed earlier, there are risks to a company such as transactional, translational and economic risk. These exposures may stem from accounting policy, corporate structure and taxation, trading partners or many other causes. It is important to establish a frequency in which the company reviews its exposures to prevent new risks from going unnoticed.

Quantify Exposures

How would a foreign exchange movement impact your known exposures and your company's financials? Quantifying your exposures can help identify the exposures with risk of most significance. There are multitudes of techniques companies utilize to measure their exposure with equally valid reasons.

Develop Risk Management Strategy

Once risks are identified and measured the next step is to create a plan of action to manage such risks. Exposures which create the most potential for risk to the company should be designated hedging. Some risks can be managed through natural hedges while others may require more complex hedging products.

Strategy Considerations:

- How will identified risks be managed?
- Which activities will be hedged?
- Which hedging products will the company be willing to accept?
- Which hedging product will be used for a particular activity?

Depending on the objectives of a risk management program, different considerations will take priority within the organization.

Implement Strategy

This step in the risk management process is to carry out the strategy outlined in the risk management plan. Identify individuals who will enter into transactions and any other contacts that need to be part of the implementation process. Clear communication within the organization is necessary to make sure the implementation strategy covers the risk mitigation needs of the company.

Internal controls are also an important consideration in the implementation strategy. Controls should be set to minimize the change of creating additional risks through the risk management process. Documentation of controls is vital for performance review.

Monitor Exposures & Hedges

Taking actions to manage risk does not end the process. Risk management monitoring must be a standard part of the process. Does the hedged amount cover the appropriate level of risk? Have needs changed as the company has better insight into their quarter or year? As new information is available the risk management team must assess how hedges fulfill the needs of the business.

Keep in mind that performance measurements may be required as part of regulation, such as FAS 133. Audit trails should be identified along with independent verification of controls for consistency. Communication must go out to management and stakeholders to avoid any surprises as the environment changes.

Review Performance

The final step in the process is to review how effectively the risk management process worked. Risk management may require continuous process improvements. By analyzing outcomes the company can finely tune its processes in order to further limit risk. Results should be documented and tracked over time to enable mandated offers to attest to the integrity of the overall integrity.

Hedge Accounting

Accounting of foreign currency risk may receive special treatment permitting that the company follows hedge accounting rules. Criteria for measuring the effectiveness of hedging must be established at the inception of the program. Hedge accounting is an important consideration when structuring the framework of foreign exchange risk management program. As part of the ongoing risk management, the company must periodically evaluate the gains or losses associated from hedging and report this in the company's earnings report.

Occurrence of a foreign exchange hedge requires the company to exclude from their assessments of hedge effectiveness the portions of the fair value of forward contracts attributable to spot-forward differences. For example, the difference between the spot and forward exchange rate.

Cash flows must be estimate cash flows from forecasted transactions based on the current spot rate. This cash flow must be adjusted for time value. The effectiveness of the hedge is then assessed by comparing the change in fair value of the forward contracts attributed to the changes in dollar spot price of the foreign currency to changes in present value of the forecasted cash flow based on the current spot rate.

8 FOREIGN EXCHANGE IN SUPPLY CHAIN

Whether or not a company is aware, most companies face foreign exchange exposure. Often time foreign exchange exposure is direct, but indirect exposure should also be identified. A common source of indirect exposure for a company resides in their supply chain.

In a simplistic supply chain model, there can be six different segments within the supply chain. Each segment may face direct foreign exchange risk. A short term foreign exchange movement may not be able to be passed through to a customer due to contract pricing and other factors. Such instance would result in possible gross margin deterioration. Over a long period of time a significant foreign exchange movement may cause industry-wide price adjustments. For purposes of this chapter only short term currency fluctuations are discussed.

Continuous Supply Chain Cycle:

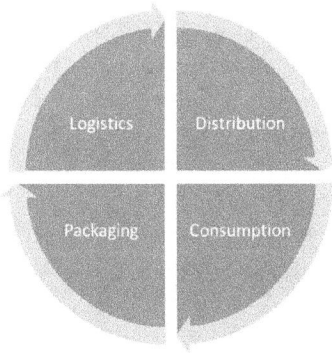

Supply Chain Components

The supply chain is a continuous cycle as shown in the previous diagram. It is a combination of packaging, logistics, distribution, and consumption. There are six different segments of the supply chain that start from the most basic raw material supplier all the way down the end consumer.

- Raw material supplier: Raw material suppliers often produce in developing countries. Input materials to extract commodities from their natural state often require a significant amount of energy to recover. Exposures from a raw material supplier consist of origin of production, location of customer, and cost of energy (such as oil) to extract materials. This segment is also an indicator of future long term price increases.

- Supplier: Suppliers may offer value-add benefits to raw materials or produce components necessary for the next segment in the supply chain. This segment must take supplier and customer location of operations in consideration of foreign exchange risk. Inventory foreign currency translation is also an important concern for this segment.

- Manufacturer: The manufacturer combines inputs to produce a product. Similar to the supplier it must consider its supplier and wholesaler locations when assessing foreign exchange risk. Internal operations may be conducted globally which can create additional exposure. Translation risk expands beyond inventory to include work in process (WIP) valuation.

- Wholesaler: A wholesaler may buy from several different manufacturers globally. Customers may also be as global as its suppliers. Wholesalers should consider input and output foreign exchange risk as well as inventory translation of its inventory abroad.

- Retailer: Similar to a wholesaler a retailer purchase products from wholesalers globally. Customers may also be as diverse.

- End customer: The end consumer faces foreign exchange risk which is passed on from the retailer.

Supply Chain Impact On COGS

Industries where margins are narrow face the most risk from a financial perspective. Companies should consider how easily foreign exchange risk can be passed downstream. Often pass-through is less than the total risk. Therefore each member of the supply chain bears some cost in regards to foreign exchange movement.

If pass-through occurs a supply chain member may look to substitute items upon a price movement. Companies should look to natural hedges in their respective operating locations and potentially hedge their net exposure through financial instruments and derivatives. In general, a company who takes ownership of the foreign exchange risk may often have better control in their exchange rate and ultimately their pricing.

Example:

	Today	Scenario 1	Scenario 2
Revenue	$ 1,000,000	$ 1,000,000	$ 1,000,000
Imported Components LC	500,000	500,000	500,000
Exchange Rate	1.25	1.15	1.35
Imported US Cost	$ 625,000	$ 575,000	$ 675,000
US Manufacturing Cost	$ 200,000	$ 200,000	$ 200,000
Total COGS	$ 825,000	$ 775,000	$ 875,000
Profit	$ 175,000	$ 225,000	$ 125,000

An adverse foreign exchange rate movement can negatively impact a company's cost of goods sold, or COGS. If operating costs increase for a business as a result of foreign exchange movement, a company may not be able to pass this cost over to their customer. The result of such impact is a narrowing of profit margin. Conversely, if the foreign exchange moves favorably for a company, they experience a more favorable margin.

The previous table compares a current market impact on the profit and loss of a company given an un-hedged exchange rate of 1.25. Notice how the profit changes as the foreign exchange rate changes.

- Scenario 1 had a positive FX move in relation to imported components.
- Scenario 2 had a negative FX move in relation to imported components.

Hedging foreign exchange risk on imported components ensures COGS stability. While a hedge limits the upside potential of a favorable foreign exchange movement, it also protects the company from less favorable market conditions.

Foreign Exchange Risk on Supply Chain Revenue

	Today	Scenario 1	Scenario 2
Revenue	1,000,000	1,000,000	1,000,000
Exchange Rate	1.25	1.15	1.35
Total Revenue	$ 1,250,000	$ 1,150,000	$ 1,350,000
Total COGS	$ 1,200,000	$ 1,200,000	$ 1,200,000
Profit	$ 50,000	$ (50,000)	$ 150,000

An adverse foreign exchange rate movement can also negatively impact revenue numbers. If a company conducts its sales in another currency then it is exposed to risk to its top line revenue. Similarly to a situation where cost of goods sold can vary, variations in the foreign exchange rate can alter revenue once translated into the functional currency of a company.

The table above shows how the change in foreign exchange rate can impact the bottom line of a company holding all else constant.

- Scenario 1 had a negative FX move in relation to export revenue
- Scenario 2 had a positive FX move in relation to export revenue

Hedging FX risk on imported components avoids profit margin pressure. Companies with narrow margins face headwinds when operating overseas without hedging program. In the first scenario above the company actually experiences an operating loss once foreign revenue is converted to its functional currency.

Takeaway

Regardless of the positioning within a supply chain, a company may operate with foreign currency exposure. Some companies may face direct foreign exchange risk from suppliers or customers. Other companies may face foreign exchange risk indirectly. In each circumstance it is important for a company to consider the global footprint of its supply chain. A risk management program may be necessary to mitigate financial risk.

9 HEDGE STRUCTURING

Many companies do not have sufficient international exposure to justify implementing a foreign exchange hedging program. For these companies they often resort to operating in a spot-only environment. Other companies may conduct a sizeable part of their operations internationally. In the instance of a need for a foreign exchange hedging program, there are different methodologies to hedge foreign exchange risk.

The budget cycle of a company often is prime timing for implementing hedging strategies. During the budget cycle the full financials of a company are often projected to set guidance and targets both for internal and external purposes. The financial snapshot enables treasury management to estimate risks such as foreign exchange and can establish their hedging targets as part of this process.

Hedging "back to budget" is marginally a more common method for hedging compared with other processes. The company establishes its budget for the upcoming year, for example. The hedges from the prior year are rolling off the books. The hedging company enters into hedges for the upcoming year based on its budget. The hedges established for the upcoming year are locked into place based on the budget. Back to budget introduces some intra-year volatility.

Some companies may not have such accurate insight into their financials for the next full year. These companies may take a more short term approach to hedging. Hedging six months out or even quarterly are also common practices.

FX Accounting Rate

There are three common methodologies for setting the accounting rate for foreign exchange.

Methods:

- Daily spot rate: Transactions are booked at the foreign exchange market rate on the day they occur. Remeasurement of foreign exchange movement will impact financial statements through a profit and loss impact.

- Monthly average rate: Transactions are booked using a monthly average foreign exchange rate. Remeasurement of foreign exchange movement will impact both revenue profit and loss. It will also impact remeasurement profit and loss.

- Prior month end spot rate: Transactions are booked using the spot rate at the end of the prior month. Remeasurement of foreign exchange movement impacts revenue profit and loss. It will also create translation adjustment.

The different methodologies create varying effects on the financial statements of a company. Each methodology has its merits and demerits. Companies should address methodology as part of their risk management program framework.

Structuring Forecasted Cash Flow Hedging

Most companies use one of a two basic approaches to structuring their forecasted cash flow hedging programs:

- Back to Budget
- Rolling Basis

Hedging "back to budget" is marginally more common. Under a back to budget methodology a company establishes its budget for the upcoming year sometime most often in the last quarter. During this point in time the last hedges from the previous budget cycle are rolling off the books. The company enters into new hedges based on its forecasted budget for the future year. This repeats each budget cycle. A back to budget process creates a risk of intra-year volatility. Another point of consideration is the risk that the actual results diverge from the budget. Monitoring actual financials compared to budgeted financials can give insight to any needed adjustments to the hedging strategy.

Alternatively, a company can structure their cash flow hedging on a rolling basis. Hedging on a rolling basis is often touted as more effective at reducing earnings volatility. Under a rolling basis hedging program, the company hedges the next four quarters. As each quarter rolls of the books, the company hedges out one more quarter. At any point in time there are always four quarters of hedges on the books. Rolling basis without layering doesn't meaningfully reduce inter-year or year to year volatility, it just lags it.

Rolling & Layered Approach to Hedging

Back to budget and rolling basis are basic structured forecast hedging programs. However they both do not reduce inter-year or year to year volatility. Another methodology which helps address this issue is known as a rolling and layered approach. Dollar cost averaging is known to smooth the impact of market movements on portfolios of assets and has a similar impact on a portfolio of currency risk.

A rolling and layered approach begins by hedging future quarters out. However, the percentage hedged is reduced as time goes out.

Example:

A company hedges its next four quarters which reflects its upcoming year based on its current budget.

- The first quarter is hedged 100%.
- The second quarter is hedged 75%.
- The third quarter is hedged 50%.
- Finally the fourth quarter is hedged 25%.

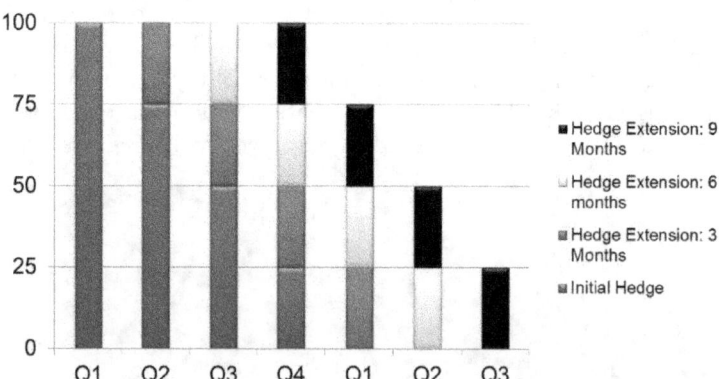

As the quarters progress, the company hedges the remaining portion of the quarters incrementally twenty five percent.

- The second quarter is hedged an additional 25%.
- The third quarter is hedged an additional 25%.
- The fourth quarter is hedged an additional 25%.
- The first quarter of the next year is hedged an additional 25%.

This process continues throughout the year. Eventually each quarter becomes comprised of four separate layers of hedges from prior periods. The result is an average weighted hedge for each quarter.

Layering hedges a greater percentage of forecast cash flow in the near periods than the far periods and adds layers as time passes. The process was introduced by firms to manage forecast error but with the very beneficial effect of introducing dollar cost averaging. By using a rolling with layering approach, companies are rarely buying/selling currency pairs at the market's highs or lows but rather trending with the market and reducing the variability of its effective exchange rate.

PART III: FOREIGN EXCHANGE IN PRACTICE

WILLIAM THOMAS

10 FOREIGN EXCHANGE IN PRACTICE

In previous sections we discussed the basics of foreign exchange and some basic tools available to hedge. Assuming a company has a foreign exchange exposure, what is the next step? In this chapter different scenarios and the execution of different hedging products to mitigate certain foreign exchange risks will be discussed. The examples provided are used to help explain how different tools can be leveraged to mitigate an exposure and are not all encompassing solutions for a foreign exchange risk.

Initial Considerations

Before covering an exposure there are some questions that need to be answered. Keep these in mind as a basic framework in helping to decide what to communicate when entering into a foreign exchange transaction.

Questions:

- Do you intend to buy or sell the foreign currency?
- Do you use American or European terms? *
- Is the transaction for value spot or will you be covering a future transaction?

- If covering a future transaction, how confident are you that the foreign currency transaction will need to occur in the future?

* Most US commercial banks quote currencies in European terms so it is important to make sure how you are reporting your transactions.

Different products may be quoted at different exchange rates. Before making a decision it is recommended to compare all options available and the cost-benefit tradeoff between each decision. The more flexible the terms of a trade the less favorable overall rate you typically would see.

11 SPOT MARKET

The spot transaction is the most basic risk management tool outside of utilizing natural hedges. Earlier in the reading the "bid-offer" spread was discussed. Depending on which side of the market the exchange takes place the rate will vary. It is also important to know the standard market convention for a currency to avoid 'doubling up' on a currency. The best way to avoid confusion is to have clear communication throughout the dealing process. The following examples will provide four different scenarios for a spot transaction. The first two examples provide the perspective of an importer and exporter for currencies quoted in European terms. For the second two examples both the importer and exporter will transaction in currencies in American terms.

European Terms

For an Importer

Company XYZ is an importer based in the U.S. It purchases widgets from a Japanese supplier and sells them domestically in the U.S. marketplace. The company's supplier quotes its terms of trade in Japanese Yen. The invoice for this month's shipment is ¥ 80,000,000 due immediately.

Interbank Market Rates for JPY

CCY	Bid	Offer
JPY	87.50	87.60

Company XYZ needs to purchase Japanese Yen from the bank and deliver the currency immediately to its supplier. Recall that the Yen is reported European terms so the pairing is quoted as USD / JPY. The base currency is USD. The bank buys the base currency at the bid (USD) and sells the foreign currency. Therefore the rate that Company XYZ would receive from the bank for their request would be 87.50, or 87.50 Japanese Yen per US Dollar.

Calculation:

Payable (JPY):	¥ 80,000,000
USD/JPY Exchange Rate:	87.50
USD Equivalent	$914,285.71

To simplify the transaction we will assume that a standard spot transaction will be sufficient to pay the invoice. The Yen payable amount is divided by the exchange rate to get to the US dollar amount. The current market rate implies that Company XYZ will need to pay the bank USD 914,285.71 to receive JPY 80,000,000 to be sent to the supplier for payment.

For an Exporter

Let us now assume that Company XYZ is an exporter of widgets. Company XYZ is an exporter based in the U.S. and it sells widgets to a retail conglomerate in Mexico. The customer in Mexico wishes to purchase MXN 12,800,000.00 worth of widgets from Company XYZ. Payment to Company XYZ will be in for form of Mexican Pesos in this transaction.

Interbank Market Rates for MXN

CCY	Bid	Offer
MXN	12.800	12.850

Company XYZ would like its funds to be converted into US dollars once they receive the payment. The standard market convention for Mexican Pesos is USD / MXN. Therefore the rate that Company XYZ would receive from the bank for their request would be on the bank's offer, or 12.850. The company will purchase USD at 12.850 pesos per dollar.

Calculation:

Receivable (MXN):	12,800,000.00
USD/MXN Exchange Rate:	12.800
USD Equivalent	$1,000,000.00

Once again we will assume that a standard spot transaction will be sufficient to pay the invoice. The Pesos receivable amount is divided by the exchange rate to get to the US dollar amount. Company XYZ will receive $1,000,000.00 from the bank in exchange for its MXN 12,800,000.00 receivable.

American Terms

For an Importer

Company XYZ is an importer based in the U.S. It purchases widgets from an Australian supplier. The company's supplier quotes its terms of trade in Australian Dollars. The invoice for this month's shipment is AUD 1,000,000 due immediately.

Interbank Market Rates for AUD

CCY	Bid	Offer
AUD	1.0450	1.0500

Company XYZ needs to purchase Australian Dollars from the bank and deliver the currency immediately to its supplier. The Australian Dollar is quoted in American terms so the pairing is quoted as AUD / USD. The base currency is AUD. The bank buys the base currency at the bid (AUD) and sells the US dollar. Therefore the rate that Company XYZ would receive from the bank for their request would be 1.0500, or 1.0500 US Dollar per Australian dollar.

Calculation:

Payable (AUD):	1,000,000
AUD/USD Exchange Rate:	1.0500
USD Equivalent	$1,050,000.00

The AUD payable amount is multiplied by the exchange rate to get to the US dollar amount. The current market rate implies that Company XYZ will need to pay the bank USD 1,050,000.00 to receive AUD 1,000,000.00 to be sent to the supplier for payment.

For an Exporter

Conversely, let us now assume that Company XYZ is an exporter of widgets. The company received an order request from a customer in Germany. The customer wishes to purchase EUR 1,000,000.00 worth of widgets from Company XYZ. Company XYZ will be the recipient of Euro in this transaction which it will want to convert to US dollars.

Interbank Market Rates for EUR

CCY	Bid	Offer
EUR	1.3500	1.3550

The Euro is quoted in American terms so the pairing is quoted as EUR / USD. The base currency is the Euro. Company XYZ will sell EUR and purchase USD so it will be on the left-hand (bid) side of the market. Therefore the rate that Company XYZ would receive from the bank for their request would be 1.3500, or 1.3500 US Dollar per Euro.

Receivable (EUR):	1,000,000.00
EUR/USD Exchange Rate:	1.3500
USD Equivalent	$1,350,000.00

Once again we will assume that the client has received the funds and will enter into a standard spot transaction. The EUR payable amount is multiplied by the exchange rate to get to the US dollar amount. Company XYZ will sell its incoming funds of EUR 1,000,000.00 to the bank and receive US dollars for a US equivalent of $1,350,000.00.

WILLIAM THOMAS

12 FORWARD CONTRACT

Building upon the spot transaction, sometimes the payment or receipt of money does not take place immediately. Companies can offer varying payment terms that can last for a month or longer. If the transaction takes place at a future point in time, the company may want to lock in an exchange rate today to avoid a less favorable foreign exchange rate down the road. The client should consider entering into a forward transaction to hedge their potential foreign exchange risk.

Definition

A forward contract is a purchase or sale of one currency against another for a single value date (delivery) greater than the spot value date. The exchange rate is calculated by adding or subtracting forward swap points, depending on interest rate differentials, to the current spot rate.

- Premium - If the all-in price of the exchange rate is greater than the current spot it is said to trade at a forward premium.

- Discount - If the all-in price of the exchange rate is less than the current spot exchange rate it is said to trade at a forward discount.

Uses

Forward contracts are used to lock in an exchange rate for a known cash flow to be received at a specific future point in time. It can be used to lock in an exchange rate for a future payable or receivable. Locking in rates can provide corporations stability in their forecasts.

Forward Outright

The most basic forward contract is called a forward outright, or deliverable forward contract. A forward outright contract locks in a rate for a specific future date in time. Remember that a forward is defined as any point in time beyond spot settlement for a transaction. This means that any transaction over the typical two day settlement, or one day in the case of Canada, will require a forward contract.

European Terms

For an Importer

Recall in our previous example that Company XYZ purchases widgets from a Japanese supplier and has an invoice for this month's shipment of ¥ 80,000,000. Instead of the payment due immediately, we will now say that the payment is due one month from   today.

Interbank Market Rates for JPY

CCY	Bid	Offer
Spot	87.50	87.60
Points	-2.50	-2.10

Company XYZ needs to purchase Japanese Yen one month forward from the bank and deliver the currency to its supplier. Notice how forward points are quoted along with the spot rate. The forward points are an adjustment to the spot rate to account for the interest rate movement during the life of the forward contract. The points are negative in this example so it is considered a forward discount.

The exchange rate will follow the same side of the market as the initial spot transaction earlier. Company XYZ wants to purchase JPY to make their future payment obligation. The exchange rate will be the sum of the spot rate plus forward points. This would imply that the exchange rate for this transaction will be 87.50 – 2.50, or 85.00 Japanese Yen per US Dollar. The exchange rate for a spot transaction was 87.50 implying less Yen will be received for the same amount of dollars.

Calculation:

Payable (JPY):	¥ 80,000,000
USD/JPY Exchange Rate:	85.00
USD Equivalent	$ 941,176.47

Company XYZ will pay $941,176.47 today to lock in their contract for a one month payment to their supplier of ¥ 80,000,000. Recall in the spot transaction the US amount was only $914,285.71. This difference in rate accounts for the opportunity cost of holding the equivalent amount of interest for the one month period.

For an Exporter

Let us now assume that Company XYZ is an exporter of widgets and it sells widgets to a retail conglomerate in Mexico. The customer in Mexico plans to purchase MXN 12,800,000.00 worth of widgets from Company XYZ and make payment in one month.

Interbank Market Rates for MXN

CCY	Bid	Offer
Spot	12.800	12.850
Points	0.050	0.055

Company XYZ needs to sell Mexican Pesos one month forward from the bank and convert the Pesos to US dollars. The forward points in this example are at a premium to the spot market. The exchange rate will follow the same side of the market as the initial spot transaction earlier so they will be on the right-hand side. The exchange rate for this transaction will be 12.850 + 0.055, or 12.905 Mexican Pesos per US Dollar. The exchange rate for a spot transaction was 12.850 implying more Pesos will be paid for the same amount of dollars.

Calculation:

Receivable (MXN):	12,800,000.00
USD/MXN Exchange Rate:	12.905
USD Equivalent	$ 991,863.62

Company XYZ will receive $ 991,863.62 in one month time when the Pesos are exchanged for US dollars. This compares to $1,000,000.00 with a spot transaction. Once again this different in US dollar equivalent has to do with the interest rate differential between the currencies.

American Terms

<u>For an Importer</u>

Company XYZ purchases widgets from an Australian supplier. The invoice for this month's shipment is AUD 1,000,000 due in one month.

Interbank Market Rates for AUD

CCY	Bid	Offer
Spot	1.0450	1.0500
Points	-.0250	-.0200

Company XYZ needs to purchase Australian Dollars for one month forward. As with the spot transaction the company will purchase AUD on the right-hand side. The all-in forward rate for the transaction will be 1.0500 – 0.0200, or 1.0300 US Dollar per Australian dollar.

Calculation:

Payable (AUD):	1,000,000
AUD/USD Exchange Rate:	1.0300
USD Equivalent	$1,030,000.00

The current forward rate implies that Company XYZ will need to pay the bank USD 1,030,000.00 to receive AUD 1,000,000.00 to be sent to the supplier for payment. In the spot transaction recall that they company needed to pay USD 1,050,000.00.

<u>For an Exporter</u>

As an exporter, Company XYZ will receive EUR 1,000,000.00 in one month. The company will want to convert to US dollars. Company XYZ will enter a one month forward contract to sell EUR against dollars.

Interbank Market Rates for EUR

CCY	Bid	Offer
Spot	1.3500	1.3550
Points	0.0100	0.0150

Company XYZ will sell EUR and purchase USD so it will be on the left-hand (bid) side of the market. Therefore the rate that Company XYZ would receive from the bank for their request would be 1.3500 + 0.0100, or 1.3600 US Dollar per Euro.

Receivable (EUR):	1,000,000.00
EUR/USD Exchange Rate:	1.3600
USD Equivalent	$1,360,000.00

Company XYZ will sell its incoming funds of EUR 1,000,000.00 to the bank and receive US dollars for a US equivalent of $1,360,000.00. This compares to the $1,350,000.00 quoted for a spot transaction.

Forwards in Summary

For market speculators, forward contracts are an effective way benefit from a potential future market movement. For corporate hedgers, deliverable forward contracts are an effective hedging tool when conducting trade in foreign currency. The downside of a deliverable forward contract is the reliance on trading only on the maturity date. However, the cash flow is perfectly hedged from the initiate of the contract until contract maturity. By locking in an exchange rate for a known future cash flow, companies can improve their forecasting process and protect their operating margins.

13 OPTION DATE FORWARD CONTRACT

A forward contract creates a fixed foreign exchange rate between two currencies at a specific future date. What if a company is uncertain when the funds will arrive? An option date forward contract may be the right choice in such instance.

The difference between a forward and an option date forward is a contract window. A contract window creates a length of time which the rate can be utilized. At any time during the window a client can exchange their currency up to the agreed amount. An option date forward contract creates flexibility when a payment or receipt is known to exist without a definitive date.

Example:

From a previous example, Company XYZ will be receiving EUR 1,000,000.00 for an order they fulfilled to a customer in Germany. The terms of trade provided XYZ's customer thirty days, or one month, to make payment. The deal thus far is the same as the forward example previously discussed. Now assume that the client frequently pays its obligation two weeks early. Company XYZ does not know exactly which day they will receive the Euros but knows it possibly will arrive earlier than thirty days. XYZ wishes to convert EUR to USD as quickly as possible to meet its own obligations and does not want to wait a full thirty days before converting the funds.

Company XYZ will enter into a one month forward contract with a two week window. The contract allows the company to drawdown on the forward contract during the last two weeks of the contract period.

Interbank Market Rates for EUR

CCY	Bid	Offer
Spot	1.3500	1.3550
Points: 2 Weeks	0.0050	0.0080
Points: 4 Weeks	0.0100	0.0150

Once again the spot portion of the contract will be on the bid because this is where the bank buys Euros against dollars. Notice how two quotes are given for forward points in the table. Because Company XYZ has a timeframe which it looks to drawdown on the contract, the bank is uncertain whether the company will ask to convert Euros to dollars in two or four weeks. The bank will look at the worst case scenario to determine the forward points. Because the points are at a premium, the rate will include the least amount of points in exchange for US dollars. Therefore the all-in exchange rate would be 1.3500 + 0.0050, or 1.3550.

Receivable (EUR):	1,000,000.00
EUR/USD Exchange Rate:	1.3550
USD Equivalent	$1,355,000.00

Company XYZ will lock in the rate at 1.3550 and will be able to sell its Euros to the bank any time during the last two weeks of the one month window. The company will sell EUR 1,000,000.00 and receive $1,355,000.00. Notice how this is less than the $1,360,000.00 that the company would otherwise receive because of the interest rate differential during the two week period.

Conversely, if Company XYZ were buying Euros against dollars (i.e. as an importer) the spot would be on the right-hand (offer) side and the four week forward points would be used. The all-in for buying Euros would be 1.3550 + 0.0150, or 1.3700.

Option Dated Forwards in Summary

If a market speculator or corporate hedger knows a reasonable window of time as to which they will have a known amount of cash flow, an option dated window may be better suited to hedge. An option dated window locks in a foreign currency exchange rate for a period of time which can be drawn down upon. Although an option dated window may offer a less favorable rate compared to a regular forward contract, the flexibility of an option dated window can be appealing when the exact timing of cash flow is unknown.

14 COMPENSATING CONTRACT

A compensating contract is a foreign exchange contract where a contract is used to offset some of the obligation of an existing contract. A typical compensation transaction completely offsets one currency in the transaction with no delivery by either party. The second currency is delivered in full, or netted, with the difference delivered to one of the parties.

There are a few common characteristics in a compensating contract. A compensating contract must call for the exchange of the same two currencies as the initial contract and have the same value date. The compensating contract should also contain a reference to the existing contract to avoid confusion.

Example:

Recall that Company XYZ will be receiving EUR 1,000,000.00 for an order they fulfilled to a customer in Germany. The company entered into an outright one month forward contract with the bank at the rate of 1.3550. Let us now assume that the customer decides to cancel their order. The change has created a EUR 1,000,000.00 exposure for Company XYZ because of their existing forward contract. The excess Euros are unneeded and the company decides to enter into a compensating contract to fully offset its Euro contract amount.

Company XYZ will enter into a one month forward contract where they buy EUR 1,000,000.00. This is because the Euro is the currency the company wishes to net fully against in the contract. The settlement of difference between the two contracts will be in US dollars.

Interbank Market Rates for EUR

CCY	Bid	Offer
Spot	1.3200	1.3250
Points	0.0025	0.0030

The market has moved since the initial forward contract was entered. The bank offers EUR 1,000,000.00 at the initial contract's expiration at a current rate of 1.3250 + 0.0030, or 1.3280. The transaction flow and netting of contracts can be seen below.

Company XYZ

	CCY	Amount		Rate		CCY	Amount
Sold	EUR	-1,000,000.00	@	1.3550	for	USD	$1,355,000.00
Bought	EUR	1,000,000.00	@	1.3280	for	USD	-$1,328,000.00
Net	EUR	0.00			for	USD	$27,000.00

Notice how the US Dollar appreciated against the Euro since the initial contract. Because Company XYZ is buying Euros on the compensating contract with a stronger dollar, the company does not have to pay as much to offset the contract. The net result is a positive balance of USD 27,000.00 to be paid to Company XYZ by the bank.

Compensating Contract in Summary

A compensating contract is a valuable tool to exit out of an existing forward contract. It provides flexibility for a trader or corporate hedger when a change in the environment occurs. A compensating contract can result in a short term liability. However, the elimination of an unnecessary forward contract can surpass the cost of unwinding the deal.

15 PARTIAL OFFSET CONTRACT

The same theory can be applied to a partial offset to an existing contract. Let us now assume that the customer renegotiated terms of the transaction instead of cancelling. The new terms of the contract are to pay EUR 800,000.00 for the same delivery. The change in payment due has created a EUR 200,000.00 exposure in their existing forward contract. The company does not need to sell as many Euros and decides to enter into a compensating contract to reduce its overall reduction of the future contract.

Company XYZ will enter into a forward contract where they buy EUR 200,000.00.

Interbank Market Rates for EUR

CCY	Bid	Offer
Spot	1.3200	1.3250
Points	0.0025	0.0030

The market has moved since the initial forward contract was entered. The bank will sell EUR 200,000.00 at the initial contract's expiration at a rate of 1.3250 + 0.0030, or 1.3280. The transaction flow and netting of contracts can be seen below.

Company XYZ

	CCY	Amount		Rate		CCY	Amount
Sold	EUR	-1,000,000.00	@	1.3550	for	USD	$1,355,000.00
Bought	EUR	200,000.00	@	1.3280	for	USD	-$265,600.00
Net	**EUR**	**-800,000.00**			**for**	**USD**	**$1,089,400.00**

The purchase of Euros nets against the initial contract. Company XYZ now has a net forward contract of EUR 800,000.00 which perfectly matches the new terms of the payment agreement with its customer. We can calculate the implied foreign exchange rate based on the two deals.

Amount of Dollars	1,089,400.00
Amount of Euros	800,000.00
EUR / USD Implied Rate	1.36175

The purchase of Euros at a new market rate changes the implied foreign exchange rate. The implied rate of 1.31675 is higher than the initial contract of 1.3550. To put it differently, Company XYZ will receive a more favorable rate of exchange (more US dollars per Euro) under the netting of contracts.

Partial Offset Contract in Summary

A partial offset contract can be used to reduce the position of an existing hedge. By entering into a reduced position in the opposite direction of the existing hedge, the result is a lower overall position in the forward contract. Similarly to a compensating contract, a partial offset contract is another tool used to help manage exposure.

16 SWAP CONTRACT

A foreign exchange swap contract is an agreement between two parties where there is a simultaneous purchase and sale of identical amounts of one currency for another at two different points in time. A swap consists of two parts known as 'legs'. There is both a near leg and far leg in the transaction. The near leg is either a spot or forward transaction. The far leg takes place at a date beyond the near leg and offsets the initial trade. A forward-forward transaction is a common swap which will be discussed at a later point.

There are several ways a swap can be used. The most common use of a swap is for institutions, such as banks, to manage positions, currency account balances or to take advantage of interest rate arbitrage opportunities. Swaps can be used to alter the settlement timing of an existing forward contract (early settlement or extension).

Examples of a Swap

- Early settlement of a forward contract
- 'Rolling' (extending) a forward contract
- Borrowing / lending foreign currency account balances
- Forward-forward transaction

Early Settlement

<u>For an Importer</u>

Recall in the outright forward example earlier Company XYZ is an importer of widgets from an Australian supplier. The invoice for this month's shipment is AUD 1,000,000 due in one month. Now assume that the Australian supplier has delivered the product two weeks early. Company XYZ must pay the invoice earlier than the foreign exchange contract they entered into with the bank. The company can enter into a swap contract against its existing forward contract.

Interbank Market Rates for AUD

CCY	Bid	Offer
Spot	1.0430	1.0470
Points	-.0120	-.0100

On the near leg of the swap, the bank will sell AUD at a spot value of 1.0470 to Company XYZ for US 1,047,000.00. Simultaneously, the bank will repurchase the Australian dollars in two weeks at the rate of 1.0470 - .0120, or 1.0350. Notice how the bid-side points were used.

Calculation:

Deal		CCY	Amount		Rate	CCY	Amount
Initial	Bought	AUD	1,000,000.00	@	1.0300	USD	-$1,030,000.00
Swap Near	Bought	AUD	1,000,000.00	@	1.0470	USD	-$1,047,000.00
Swap Far	Sold	AUD	-1,000,000.00	@	1.0350	USD	$1,035,000.00
	Net	**AUD**	**1,000,000.00**			**USD**	**-$1,042,000.00**

Notice how the Australian dollar amount nets to the initial amount of the contract. There is, however, a difference in the US dollar amount to be paid to the bank. Instead of $1,030,000.00 initially entered, the revised amount is now $1,042,000.00 creating an additional $12,000.00 due from Company XYZ to be paid to the bank for settlement. Keep in mind that entering into a swap position for this deal saves the company forward points for the additional two weeks although the spot market has moved less favorably to the company. The contract also avoids risks attributed to making the payment at the later date.

Rolling a Forward Contract

A swap may be used to extend an initial contract. This is in contrast to the previous example of settling a contract early. Now assume that the shipment was delayed by one month. Company XYZ needs to extend their initial one month outright forward to another month.

Interbank Market Rates for AUD

CCY	Bid	Offer
Spot	1.0430	1.0470
Points	-.0250	-.0200

The near leg of the swap will be for the value date of the initial outright forward contract. Company XYZ will sell to the bank AUD 1,000,000.00 and simultaneously repurchase the same amount for one month out. The company will sell the bank Australian dollars on the bid of 1.0430 to compensate for the initial trade. The new contract to purchase Australian dollars one month out will be at the rate of 1.0430 -.0200, or 1.0230.

Calculation:

Deal		CCY	Amount		Rate	CCY	Amount
Initial	Bought	AUD	1,000,000.00	@	1.0300	USD	-$1,030,000.00
Swap Near	Sold	AUD	-1,000,000.00	@	1.0430	USD	$1,043,000.00
Swap Far	Bought	AUD	1,000,000.00	@	1.0230	USD	-$1,023,000.00
	Net	AUD	1,000,000.00			USD	-1,010,0000.00

The Australian dollar amount nets to the initial amount of the contract. The swap has reduced the amount of US dollars owed to the bank by $20,000. The new implied foreign exchange rate for the far leg of the swap can be calculated below.

Amount of Dollars	1,010,000.00
Amount of Australian Dollars	1,000,000.00
AUD / USD Implied Rate	1.0100

Once again, entering into a swap position for this deal creates new forward points based on the addition month of time. The market has moved favorably for Company XYZ, but this is not always the case.

Borrowing / Lending Foreign Currency Account Balances

If a company holds a significant balance in one currency it can enter into a swap contract to gain the use of second currency to meet short term needs. This is known as borrowing or lending a foreign currency account balance. Although there is no loan involved, the use of currency is traded with counterparty for a short term basis.

Example:

Company XYZ has a Japanese Yen account in a bank in Tokyo, Japan. The account is used to support local payables and receivables in the company. XYZ has held a surplus balance in the account. The company does not see a need for the balance at this time but does not want to repatriate the funds back to the US because of deferred tax liabilities. However, the factory in the U.S. is in need of short term cash to build inventory for an upcoming order. The factory requests USD 2,000,000.00 for duration of one month.

The foreign exchange advisors at the bank suggest entering into a one month swap contract with the Japanese Yen available in their foreign currency account. Company XYZ will sell Yen and purchase USD 2,000,000.00 at the current spot rate. Simultaneously the company will sell USD against JPY for one month forward.

Interbank Market Rates for JPY

CCY	Bid	Offer
Spot	87.50	87.60
Points	-2.60	-2.20

Company XYZ sells JPY at the rate of 87.60 for spot value to the bank on the near leg. On the far leg the company will repurchase the JPY at the rate of 87.60 − 2.60, or 85.00 for one month.

Deal		CCY	Amount	Rate	CCY	Amount
Swap Near	Sold	JPY	-175,200,000	@ 87.60	USD	$2,000,000.00
Swap Far	Bought	JPY	170,000,000	@ 85.00	USD	-$2,000,000.00
	Net	**JPY**	**-5,200,000**		**USD**	**0.00**

The company will pay the bank JPY 175,200,000 to be delivered in two days. In one month the company will receive JPY 170,000,000 back to their foreign currency account. A swap transaction to borrow or lend a foreign currency enables a company to maintain a net position in a preferred currency and use another currency for a period of time (one month in this example). There is a slight cost of JPY 5,200,000 which will be offset by the benefit of investing the USD for the period.

Forward-Forward

When a swap consists of two forward contracts, it is called a forward-forward swap. Forward-forward swaps can be used to roll over existing forward contracts that have not yet matured. A forward-forward swap is similar to other swaps with a near leg and far leg component.

Example:

Company XYZ enters into a one month forward contract to buy ¥ 80,000,000 to cover an account payable. The all-in rate given to the client was 85.00 for a total of $ 941,176.47. Two weeks later the company is told that there is a delay in the manufacturing process and the product will not be available for an additional month. The payment is therefore delayed for the same period of time. There is now a one month gap between the forward contract and the liability. Company XYZ will enter into a forward-forward swap to adjust the date of the existing forward to reflect the revised payment terms.

Company XYZ will sell Yen and purchase USD 2,000,000.00 at the expiry date of the initial contract which is two weeks from today. Simultaneously the company will sell USD against JPY for six weeks forward, two weeks until the initial contract due date plus for weeks incremental.

Interbank Market Rates for JPY

CCY	Bid	Offer
Spot	88.50	88.60
Points: 2 Weeks	-2.50	-2.40
Points: 6 Weeks	-3.00	-2.90

On the near leg Company XYZ sells JPY at the rate of 88.60 – 2.40, or 86.20 in two weeks. On the far leg the company will repurchase the JPY at the rate of 88.60 – 3.00, or 85.60 for six weeks.

Deal		CCY	Amount		Rate	CCY	Amount
Initial	Bought	JPY	80,000,000	@	85.00	USD	-$941,176.47
Swap Near	Sold	JPY	-80,000,000	@	86.20	USD	$928,074.26
Swap Far	Bought	JPY	80,000,000	@	85.60	USD	-$934,579.44
	Net	JPY	80,000,000			USD	-$947,681.65

Taking into account the forward-forward swap, the company will purchase JPY 80,000,000 in six weeks and pay a total of USD 947,681.65. The implied exchange rate for the transaction can be calculated below.

Amount of Japanese Yen	80,000,000
Amount of US Dollars	947,681.65
USD / JPY Implied Rate	84.42

In this example the market rate is less favorable to the client than the initial foreign exchange contract. Another consideration for the company is to wait and conduct a spot trade for the near leg of the swap instead of entering into a forward. Because a forward-forward price is derived from the least favorable side of two swap markets for the customer, leaving the near leg a spot trade eliminates forward points on one side of the transaction. This may be the most cost effective option.

Engaging in a forward-forward swap or waiting to conduct a basic swap can be a difficult decision. The determination for a client can be very complex as it takes into account cash flow, forward points and interest rate forecasts.

Swap Contract in Summary

Swap contracts offer a significant amount flexibility when dealing with forward currency exchange rates. A swap contract can be used to finance short term cash flow needs in a different currency or modify an existing hedge. Although most commonly used by institutions, swap contracts can be powerful tools to tailor cash flow needs.

17 NON-DELIVERABLE FORWARD CONTRACT

A non-deliverable forward is an outright forward or futures contract which is a cash-settled, short-term forward contract. The market for NDF contracts developed for currencies that could not be delivered offshore. Such delivery restrictions stem from emerging markets with strict capital controls. NDF contracts are a popular instrument for corporations seeking to hedge exposure to a currency that is not internationally traded and are commonly quoted and settled in U.S. dollars.

An NDF contract has a fixing and settlement date. The fixing date is the date at which the difference between the prevailing market exchange rate and agreed upon exchange rate is calculated. The settlement date is the date by which the payment of the settlement difference is due to the party receiving payment.

The profit or loss of the contract is determined at the time of settlement and is calculated by taking the difference between the agreed upon exchange rate and the spot rate at the time of settlement. NDF contracts are frequently used on a thinly traded or non-convertible foreign currency.

Elements to NDF Contract:

1. Notional amount
2. Fixing date
3. Settlement date
4. Contracted NDF rate
5. Prevailing spot rate

The notional amount of an NDF is never exchanged. The only exchange of cash flows is the difference between the exchange rates between the agreed upon exchange rate and the spot rate at the time of settlement. An NDF is a "non-cash" item which is not carried on the balance sheet. NDF contracts bear lower counterparty risk.

NDF Contract in Summary

A non-deliverable forward contract is a common tool for corporate hedgers. Although certain countries impose capital restrictions on their currency, an NDF contract enables corporations to hedge their currency exposure in such restricted countries while maintaining adherence to such country policy. NDF contracts are appealing to companies as they can be settled in their functional currency, often in U.S. dollars.

18 OPTION CONTRACT

Spot and forward contracts reduce foreign exchange risk but they also eliminate any opportunity for benefit upon a potentially favorable market move. An alternative hedging product is known as an option contract. Hedging a foreign exchange exposure with an option contract can provide an asymmetrical risk profile. That is, an option contract creates limited foreign exchange risk while creating opportunity to participate in any favorable currency movement during the life of the contract.

An option contract gives the holder the right, but not an obligation, to buy or sell a certain currency against another at/by a specific date in the future.

There are two basic option contracts:

Call option – The right, but not an obligation to buy a certain currency against another.

Put option – The right, but not an obligation to sell a certain currency against another.

An option contract has both a buyer and seller of the contract. The buyer purchases the right to exchange currency at a fixed rate for a period of time. Conversely, the seller provides the opportunity for the buyer to exchange currency upon the demand of the option buyer.

The Option Buyer

The buyer of the option pays a premium to the seller. The payment to the seller represents the only obligation of the buyer in the contract terms. The premium is known before the transaction occurs and represents the worst case scenario for the client. This is because the buyer will not act on the 'insurance' contract if the market rate is better than contract terms and will lose the premium. The option buyer has three choices of action at contract expiration.

Buyer's Choices:

- **Exercise the option:** If the current market rate is less favorable to the buyer than the option rate, the buyer will exercise the option. The buyer notifies the seller that they wish to exchange currencies at the strike price. The two parties exchange currencies per the contract terms.

- **Allow the option to expire:** If the current market rate is more favorable to the buyer than the option rate, the buyer will not exercise the option. By not exercising the option the contract will go until the end of the contract period and nothing will be done. The buyer will exchange currencies in the open market to take advantage of the better exchange rate. The premium paid to the option seller will not be recovered.

- **Offset the option:** If the option holder no longer has a need for the option prior to execution, they may want to exit out of the contract. The way to relieve the holder of the position is to sell an offsetting option. The offsetting contract will net against the existing contract and eliminate the obligation.

The Option Seller

The seller can be considered the underwriter of the insurance policy. The seller will receive a premium from the buyer without knowing whether or not the buyer will exercise the option. The best case scenario for the seller is to receive a premium and see the option contract expire. The option seller takes the most risk as it has a limited benefit, the premium, and a potentially unlimited risk potential.

Scenarios

An option contract can be either a call or put contract. Each contract has both a buyer and a seller. The implication is there are four different stances of option contracts in the foreign exchange market.

Four Different Scenarios:

- **Call Buyer:** Purchases the right, but not the obligation, to buy a currency. Buyer is considered long on the currency at the strike price.

- **Call Seller:** Sells the right, but not the obligation, to buy a currency. Seller is considered short on the currency at the strike price.

- **Put Buyer:** Purchases the right, but not the obligation, to sell a currency. Buyer is considered short on the currency at the strike price.

- **Put Seller:** Sells the right, but not the obligation, to sell a currency. Seller is considered long on the currency at the strike price.

Notice how a participant can be long or short on a currency in either a call or put option. By using a call or put on either side you can hedge a foreign exchange risk in many different ways.

Terminology

Option contracts are more complex than spot and forward transactions. Clear communication is critical when entering into a contract to prevent incorrect trades from happening. Below are important terms in option contracts that are used to define the parameters of a transaction.

Buy vs. Sell – Determines whether a party is a holder or writer of the option writer.

Call vs. Put – Determines whether a party is entering the contract for a right to buy (call) or right to sell (put) a currency.

Currency – The currency to be bought and sold in the contract.

Exercise Amount – The notional amount of currency to be exchanged.

Strike Price – The currency exchange rate desired by the option buyer.

Expiration Date – The deadline for an option buyer to exercise their right to trade at contract terms.

Premium Amount – The 'price' the buyer pays to the seller in exchange for the seller taking on the foreign exchange risk during the life of the contract.

Option Pricing

Recall that the buyer of an option contract must pay a premium to the seller. The premium cost is an important consideration when deciding between a forward and option contract. The price of the premium comprises of two components – time value and intrinsic value.

Option Premium = Time Value + Intrinsic Value

An option contract is structured for settlement at a future point in time. The further the expiration date is from today, there is a greater opportunity that the buyer will act on the option contract. Time value represents the cost associated to the length of the option contract.

Intrinsic value represents the difference between the strike price and the market price if the strike price is more advantageous to the option holder. If there is no advantage to the option holder the option contract will have no intrinsic value and the premium will only reflect time value.

Contract Type	Intrinsic Value
Call Option	= Strike Price – Market Price
Put Option	= Market Price – Strike Price

Notice how the intrinsic value differs depending on whether the option is a call or put. This is because the payoff of each type of option is different. The intrinsic value can never be less than zero because the contract holder would not exercise the contract if the rate was less favorable than the current market rate.

European vs. American Options

Option contracts come in two different styles. When an option price is given it may be quoted in American or European style. American or European styles are not the same as American or European terms. American or European option styles are different types of option contracts and do not represent the format of currency pairing.

European Option - A European option contract may only be exercised at the expiration date. The decision to execute the option is a single pre-defined point in time.

American Option - An American option may be exercised at any point in time before the expiration date.

Volatility

Volatility is a measure for variation of price over time. For option pricing, volatility is directly related to time value. An increase in volatility improves the likelihood that out-of-the-money options will become in-the-money. This close connection merits a critical examination of volatility when assessing an option contract.

There are two common methodologies to examine volatility of a currency option contract:

Actual Historical Volatility – Measurement of volatility of a currency over a historical period of time.

Implied Volatility – Value of volatility of an option contract when modeling the price of an option contract (such as with Black-Scholes Model).

In either case, assessing volatility is an important consideration in an option contract.

The Greeks

Fischer Black and Myron Scholes developed a theoretical model for pricing an option contract. It was published in the Journal of Political Economy. The Black-Scholes model gives the price of European-style options. The main idea behind the derivation was to perfectly hedge an option through the purchase and sale of the underlying asset in just the right way as to 'eliminate risk'. The hedge, known as delta hedging, is the basis for hedging strategies used by many investors. The model implies there is only one right price for an option which is calculated using the Black-Scholes model.

In the currency market, the Black-Scholes has been modified into a new model known as the Garman-Kohlhagen model. The Garman-Kohlhagen model was created to cope with the presence of two interest rates - one for each currency. The mathematical model used to price an option can also be used to compute the sensitivity of the option premium to changes in the input parameters. These sensitivity measures are commonly referred to as the "Greeks" because letters of the Greek alphabet are used.

Delta

Delta is a measurement of the rate of change of option value with respect to changes in the underlying asset's price. The value of delta ranges from 0.0 to 1.0 for a long call and -1.0 to 0.0 for a long put. An at-the-money option will have a delta of 0.5 (or 50%). When used in a pricing model, the value of delta can help determine the amount of currency required to hedge the exposure. Delta can be thought of as the probability of exercise at expiration.

Gamma

Gamma measures the rate of change in the delta with respect to changes in the underlying price. It is considered a second-order Greek. Gamma measures how quickly the delta with change with movements of the underlying exchange rate. As gamma increases, the hedge will have to be adjusted more frequently. The closer the strike price gets to the market rate, the higher the gamma.

Vega

Vega measures the sensitivity to volatility with respect to the volatility of the underlying asset. Although vegas in not a Greek letter, it is an important part of the "Greeks" in option modeling. Volatility changes can result in a change in premium therefore making vega a measurement of sensitivity. It is typically expressed as the amount of money per underlying that the option's value will gain or lose as volatility changes by 1%.

Theta

Theta measures the sensitivity of the value of the option to the elapse of time. It is also known as time decay. Theta is typically measured as a loss of premium value associated with time over one day. Theta is highest when an option is at-the-money. It is also non-linear and quickly loses value towards expiration.

Rho

Rho measures the sensitivity to the interest rate. It is represented as the change in premium due to a 1% change in the underlying rate.

Lambda

Lambda measures the elasticity of an option. It represents the percentage change in option value per percentage change in the underlying price. It is a measure of leverage, or gearing.

Option Payoff Charts

In this chapter the structure of an option contract is discussed. The payoff profile of an option will be graphically displayed to better understand the option functionality. The horizontal and vertical line with arrows designates a zero axis. The vertical axis represents payoff and the horizontal axis represents the break-even point.

Reference Key:
1   Strike price
2   Break-even
KI   Knock-in
KO   Knock-out

Guide:

- The *strike price* (1) is the fixed price at which the owner of the option can purchase the underlying asset.

- The *break-even* (2) is the point which the foreign exchange rate in a strategy neither makes or loses money.

- The *knock-in* (KI) is the point which a latent option contract begins to function, once a certain price level is reached before expiration, as a normal option only.

- The *knock-out* (KO) is the point which an option expires worthless. A knock-out option sets a cap to the level an option can reach which favors the option holder while limiting the profit potential.

Long Call

Going long on a call option would imply that the owner has a very bullish view on the market. No other option contract takes advantage of a rising market more than a call option. The more bullish the view, the more out-of-the-money call contract should be bought. A premium is paid for being long on the contract. The premium reflects the loss on the contract in the graphic illustration up until the strike price at point 1. Notice how the premium paid represents the worst case scenario in the payoff chart. As the market increases, the profit level offsets the premium until it reaches the break-even point 2. Any point above the strike price at point 2 represents an overall profit on the contract.

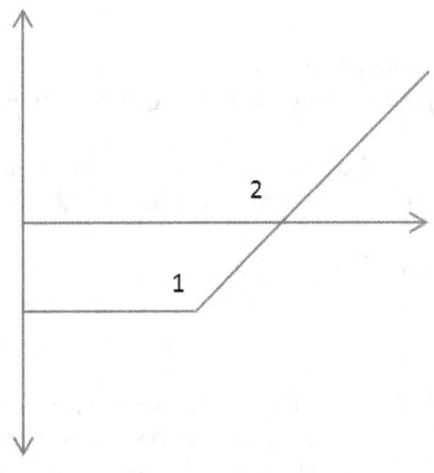

Short Call

A short call has the mirrored reflection of a long call. The short call is selling, or writing, the call contract. It reflects the other side of a long call transaction. A bearish view on the market would sell the call option and take the premium from the buyer.

If the currency falls in value then there will not be an assignment, or request from the buyer to enter into the trade. If the currency rises then the payoff will diminish the premium starting at the strike price, point 1. The full premium amount is offset by an unfavorable currency movement at the break-even, point 2. A short call has limited profit with unlimited risk.

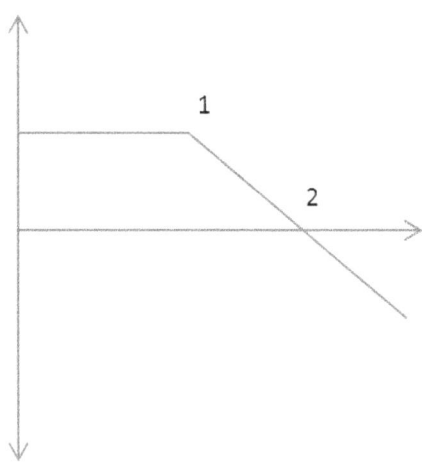

Long Put

A long put gives the right to sell a currency at a particular price. A bearish view on the market would benefit by going long on a put contract because it would profit by such movement. The transaction requires that a premium be paid to enter into the contract.

The loss is reflected up until the strike price at point 1. As the price falls below the strike price the profits offset the loss until the breakeven at point 2. The loss of the long put is limited to the premium paid.

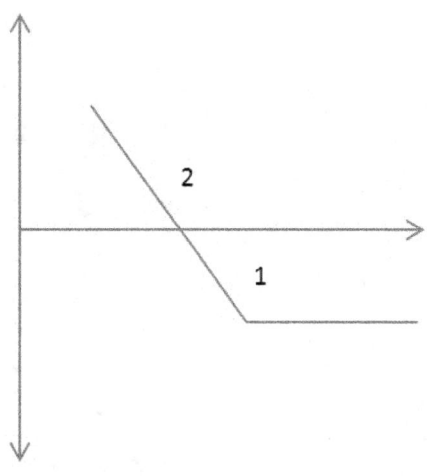

Short Put

A short put gives the right to sell the currency at a particular price. A bullish view on the market would benefit by going short on a put contract because it would receive a premium by such movement. The premium is received and represented by the profit line in the chart.

If the currency falls past the strike price, it will begin to diminish the premium up until the break-even point. A short put has limited payoff with unlimited risk.

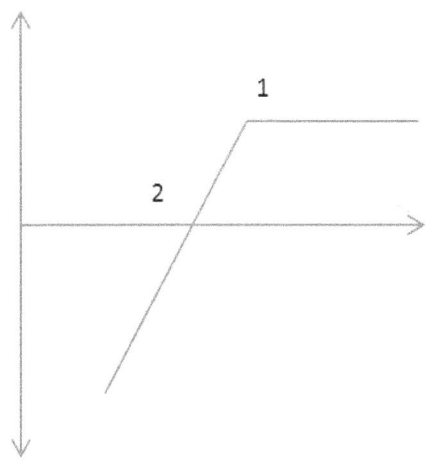

Long Straddle

A long straddle is a combination of a long call and a put at the same strike price. A view that the market will become more volatile would benefit from a long straddle position. The premium paid for the contract is reflected by a loss at point 1. As the currency moves in either direction it offsets the premium until it reaches either breakeven point. A long straddle has a limited risk profile which comes from the call-put spread premium.

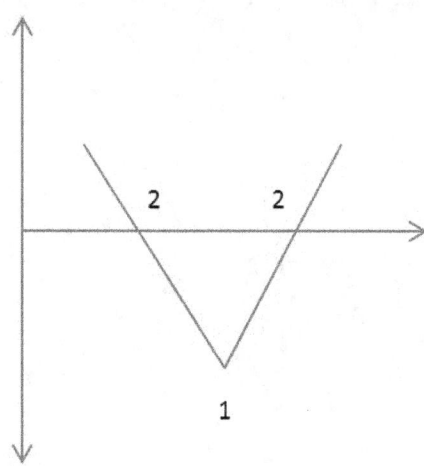

Short Straddle

A short straddle is a combination of a short call and put at the same strike price. The position benefits when volatility is stagnating. Premium is received for entering into the contract. As the currency moves in either direction it offsets the premium until it reaches either breakeven point. A short straddle has an unlimited risk with limited payoff from the premium.

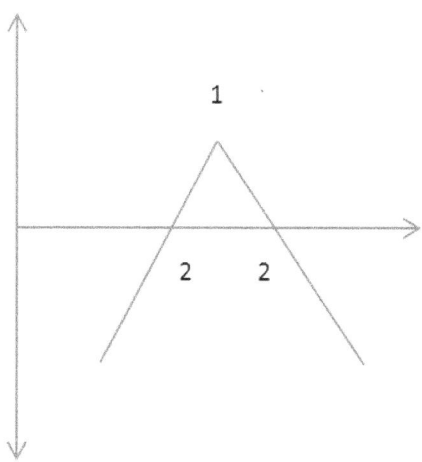

Long Strangle

The long strangle is a combination of a long put and call with a different strike price. Similarly to a long collar, a long strangle benefits in a volatile market. A premium is paid for the contract and it is reflected by a loss at both points 1. As the currency moves in either direction it offsets the premium until it reaches either breakeven point. A long strangle has a limited risk profile which comes from the call-put spread premium.

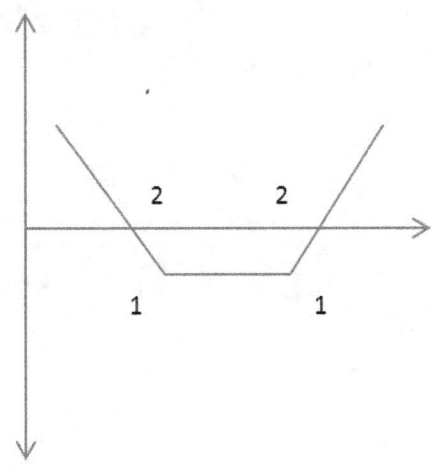

Short Strangle

A short strangle is a combination of a short call and put at different strike prices. The position benefits when volatility is stagnating. Premium is received for entering into the contract. As the currency moves in either direction it offsets the premium until it reaches either breakeven point. A short strangle has an unlimited risk with limited payoff from the premium.

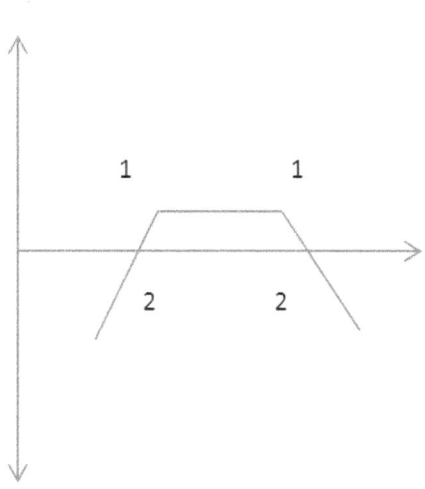

Bull Spread

A bull spread is a combination of a long and short position at a different strike price. Bull spreads can be constructed using either put or call options. The ability to use either put or call options is because of put-call parity. If the spread is created using call options it is known as a bull call spread and if it is created using put options it is known as a bull put spread. It is a bullish, vertical spread option strategy. It is designed to profit from a moderate rise in the currency. This is the most popular bullish trade. Profit and loss are both limited by the premiums on either side of the market.

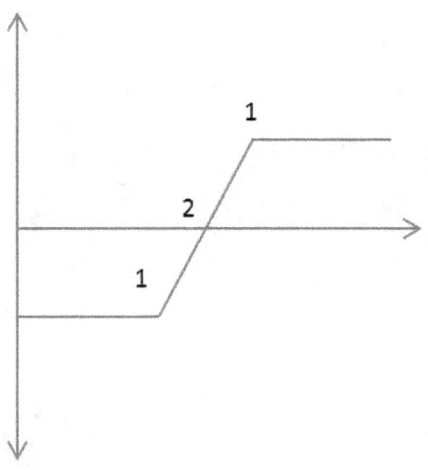

Bear Spread

A bear spread is a combination of a long and short position at a different strike price. Bear spreads can be constructed using either put or call options. If the spread is created using call options it is known as a bear call spread and if it is created using put options it is known as a bear put spread. It is a bearish, vertical spread option strategy. It is designed to profit from a moderate decline in the currency. This is the most popular bearish trade. Profit and loss are both limited by the premiums on either side of the market.

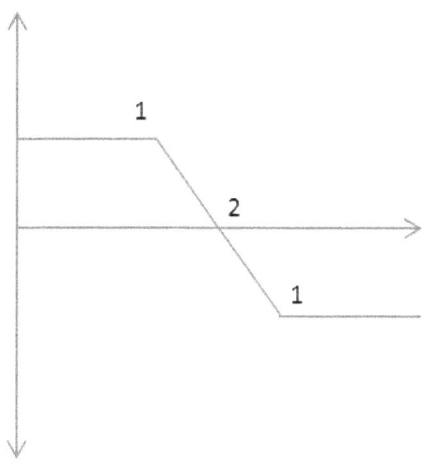

Long Butterfly

A long butterfly is a limited risk strategy designed with a high probability of earning a limited profit when future volatility is expected to be lower than implied volatility. A long butterfly position is structured with a two long calls and a short call.

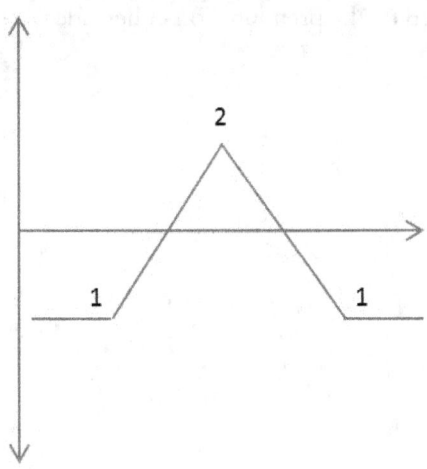

Short Butterfly

A short butterfly is a limited risk strategy designed with a high probability of earning a limited profit when future volatility is expected to be higher than implied volatility. A long butterfly position is structured with a two short calls and a long call.

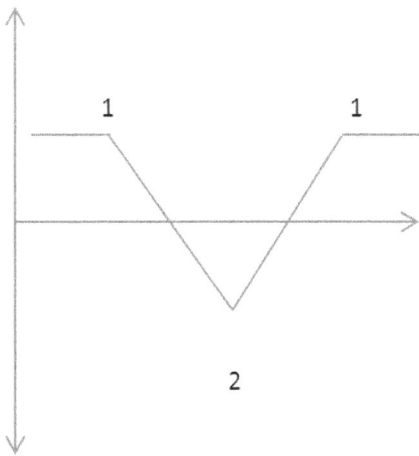

Condor

Another variation of the butterfly is called the condor. A condor is similar in structure to a butterfly. The difference between a butterfly and condor is that the condor has the middle strike of the butterfly split into two different strike prices. The payoff and risk are similar to a butterfly. Below is a graphical depiction of both a long and short condor.

Long Condor

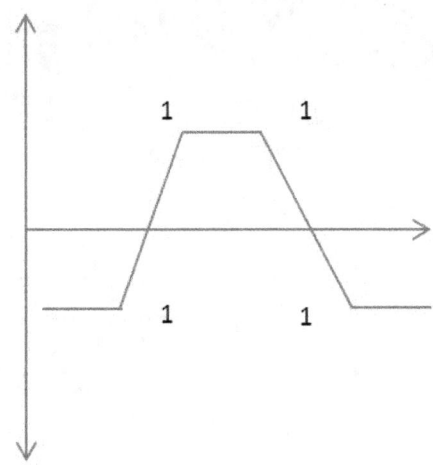

Short Condor

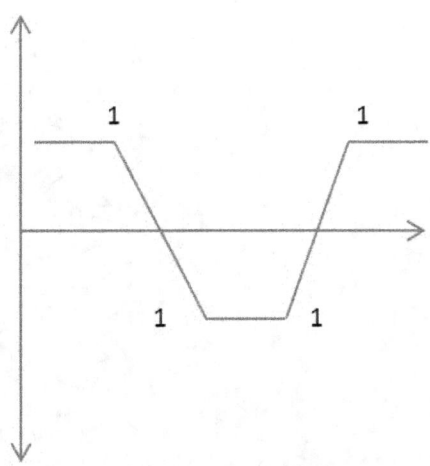

Ratio Spread

When the market is near a strike price and it is believed that a slight change in market will take place but downside protection is desired, a ratio spread should be considered. If the view is a slightly bullish, a call ratio spread can be used. If the view is slightly bearish, a put ratio can be used.

Call Ratio Spread

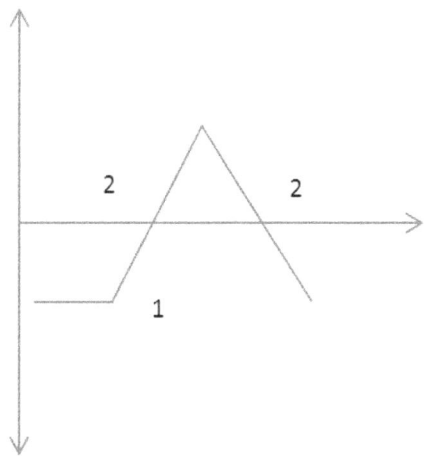

Put Ration Spread

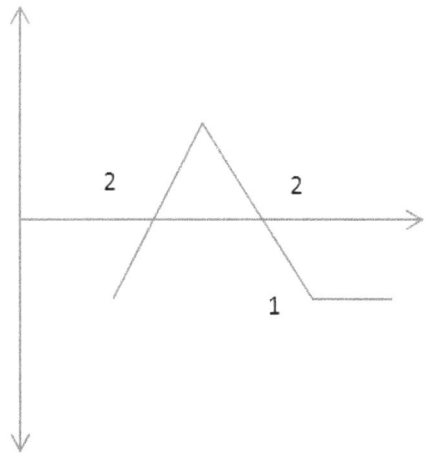

Barriers

Out-of-the-money knock-out

An out-of-the-money knock-out is a standard option that automatically cancels out if the spot rate trades through a predetermined level. The level of the knock-out is set below the initial spot rate for a call option. Conversely, the level is set above the initial spot rate for a put option.

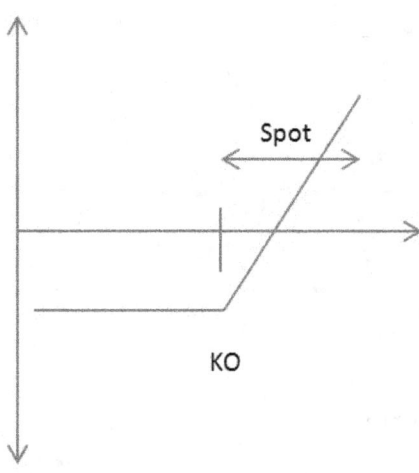

In-the-money knock-out

An in-the-money knock-out is a standard option that automatically cancels out if the spot rate trades through a predetermined level. The level of the knock-out is set above the initial spot rate for a call option. Conversely, the level is set below the initial spot rate for a put option.

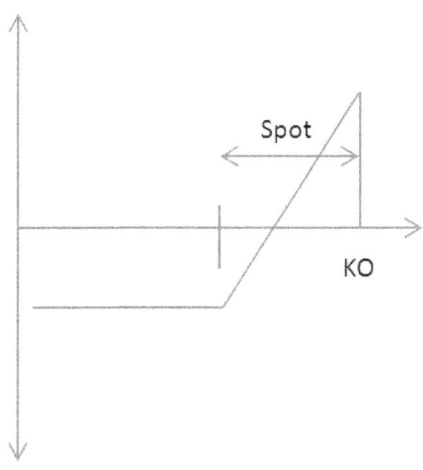

Double Knock-Out

A double knock-out is a standard option that automatically cancels out if the spot rate trades through either one or two predetermined levels. There is both an in-the-money knock-out and an out-of-the-money knock-out with this type of option. The level of the first knock-out is set above the initial spot rate. Conversely, the second knock-out level is set below the initial spot rate.

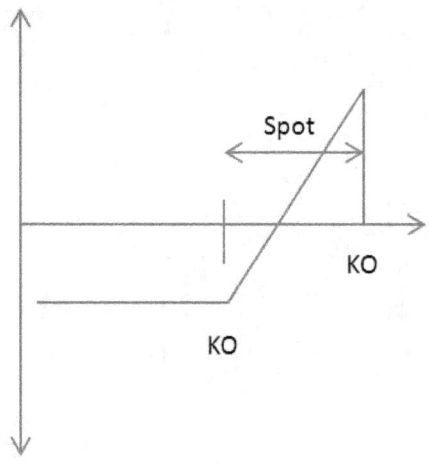

Knock-in

A knock-in option is a latent contract that takes into effect only once a certain price level is reached. For For an out-of-the-money knock-in the level is set below the initial spot for a call option and above spot for a put. For an in-the-money knock-in the level is set above the initial spot for a call option and below spot for a put.

Out-of-the-money knock-in

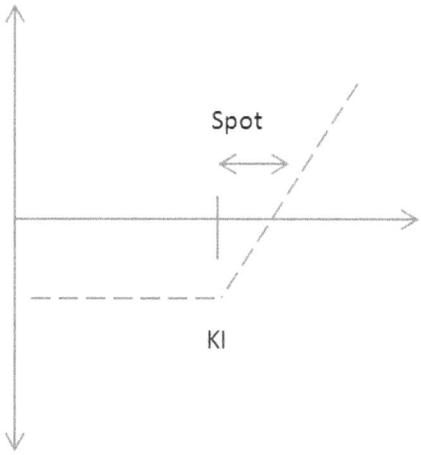

In-the-money knock-in

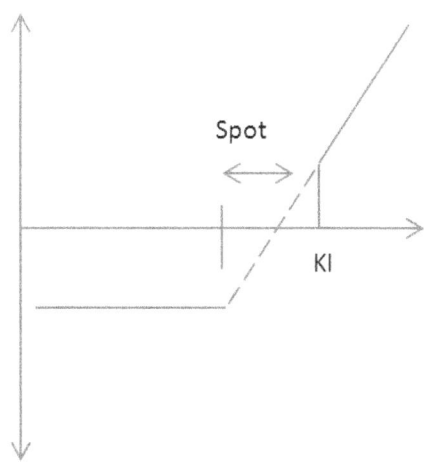

Knock-in/Knock-out

A knock-in/knock-out is an option that consists of both a knock-in and a knock-out. The option can only be exercised provided that the spot has previously traded through a defined knock-in level, and cancels out if the spot rate trades through a defined knock-out level. The knock-in is set above spot for a call and below spot for the put. The knock-out is set below the spot for the call and above the spot for the put.

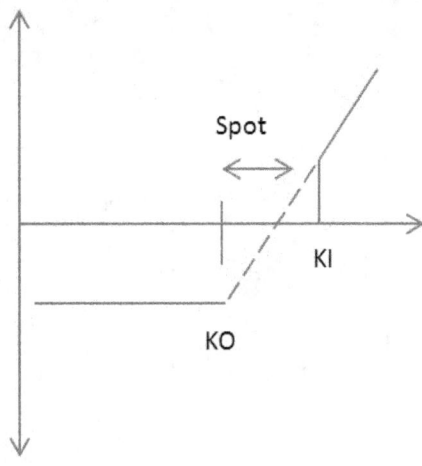

PART IV: SUMMARY

19 GLOSSARY OF TERMS

Foreign Exchange Definitions

Term	Definition
American option	An option which can be exercised at any time during the life of contract.
American terms	A foreign exchange quotation based on the number of units of U.S. dollars required in exchange for one unit of a foreign currency.
Around	Designates a forward foreign exchange rate where the bid is quoted at a discount and the offer is quoted at a premium. This can occur when the interest rate levels of two countries are identical or similar.
Assignment	Notification to the option writer requiring that party to fulfill its obligation to buy or sell the currency.
At-the-money forward	An option with an exercise price equal to the currency forward rate.

Term	Definition
At-the-money spot	An option with an exercise price equal to the currency spot rate.
Bear spread	An option strategy to take advantage of a decline of a currency with limited profit and risk.
Bid	The price at which a bank will purchase one currency in exchange for another.
Break-even point	Point which the foreign exchange rate in a strategy neither makes or loses money.
Broker	An intermediary, or agent, who arranges for the purchase or sale of foreign exchange between two parties, or the placement of Eurocurrency deposits. The broker is not at risk in the transaction.
Bull spread	An option strategy to take advantage of an increase of a currency with limited profit and risk.
Business Day	In regard to foreign exchange or Eurocurrency transactions, a day other than a Saturday or Sunday when banks in the country of each currency involved are open for business.
Butterfly spread	A butterfly is a limited risk option strategy designed with a high probability of earning a limited profit when future volatility is expected to be higher than implied volatility.
Call option	The right, but not an obligation to buy a certain currency against another.

Term	Definition
Compensation	The settlement of a foreign exchange contract by offsetting it against an opposite contract for the same value date.
Cash	A foreign exchange transaction involving the delivery of currencies on the same day that the transaction is arranged. Available early in the day for currencies of countries in the same time zone only.
Condor spread	A condor is similar in structure to a butterfly. The payoff and risk are similar to a butterfly. Below is a graphical depiction of both a long and short condor.
Cover	The purchase or sale of foreign currency to meet spot or future commitments or to close an open or short position in a foreign currency.
Cross Rate	An exchange rate between two currencies other than the U.S. dollar.
Delivery Date	See value date.
Delta	Delta is a measurement of the rate of change of option value with respect to changes in the underlying asset's price.
Direct Terms	A foreign exchange quote based on the number of units of your local currency needed in exchange for one unit of a foreign currency.
Discount	A reduction to the spot price of a currency which applies to a delivery arranged for a date other than spot.

Term	Definition
Early exercise	Settlement of a foreign currency option contract which is before the maturity date.
Exercise	Request of an option contract holder to act on the contract.
Expiration date	The last date on which the holder of the option may exercise it according to its terms.
Eurocurrency	Generally, a currency placed on deposit outside its country of origin.
Eurodollar	Generally, a U.S. dollar deposit held in a bank office (including a branch of a U.S. bank) located outside of the United States.
European option	A type of option contract which may only be exercised at the expiration date.
European terms	A foreign exchange quote based on the number of units of a foreign currency required in exchange for one U.S. dollar.
Flat	One side (bid or offer) of a swap price that is zero, meaning no adjustment to the spot price (see "Par").
Foreign Exchange Dealer	An individual who makes two-sided prices in foreign exchange and deals as a principal on behalf of his bank or other institution.
Forward-Forward Transaction	A swap where both value dates are forward dates.
Gamma	Gamma measures the rate of change in the delta with respect to changes in the underlying price.

Term	Definition
Hedging	To assume a foreign exchange position by contract or otherwise to offset an existing but opposite foreign exchange exposure.
International Monetary Market	A division of the Chicago Mercantile Exchange that provides futures markets in monetary vehicles including foreign currencies, precious metals, or other financial instruments.
Implied volatility	Value of the volatility of the underlying instrument which, when input in an option pricing model will return a theoretical value equal to the current market price of the option.
In-the-money	The derivative would make money if it were to expire today.
Indirect Terms	A foreign exchange quote based on the number of units of a foreign currency needed in exchange for one unit of your local currency.
Intrinsic value	The actual value of an underlying determined through fundamental analysis without reference to its market value.
Leads and Lags	The acceleration of receivables and the delay of disbursements due in a foreign country in which a decline in value is anticipated. Conversely, the delay of receivables and the acceleration of disbursements due in a foreign currency in which an increase in value is anticipated.

Term	Definition
Leg	Date of a forward or swap contract. Can be identified as either a near leg or far leg in a transaction.
LIBOR	Acronym for "London Interbank Offered Rate". Generally, the interbank rate for fixed date Eurodeposits traded between major banks in the London market at 11:00 a.m. London time.
Margin	A type of financial collateral used to cover credit risk.
Mark to market	Accounting for the "fair value" of an asset or liability based on the current market price.
Odd Dates	Forward dates that differ from the conventional "straight" dates such as one month, two months, etc. (e.g., six weeks, 97 days, etc.).
Offer	The price at which a bank will sell one currency in exchange for another.
Open Position	A net foreign exchange exposure that has not been offset or hedged.
Option Date Forward Contract	A specially-arranged foreign exchange forward contract that allows one of the parties a range of delivery dates at a prearranged rate.
Option Contract	A specially-arranged foreign exchange forward contract that allows one of the parties a range of delivery dates at a prearranged rate.

Term	Definition
Out-of-the-money	The derivative would not make money if it were to expire today.
Outright Forward	A simple purchase or sale of foreign exchange for a forward date. Not a swap.
Par	One side (bid or offer) of a swap price that is zero, meaning no adjustment to the spot price (see "Flat").
Point	Generally, the number "one" in the last decimal place to which a foreign exchange quote is normally carried for a given currency (e.g., an English pound spot quote of 1.7280 - 1.7290 has a spread of ten points).
Premium	An increase to the spot price of a currency which applies to a delivery arranged for a date other than spot.
Put option	The right, but not an obligation to sell a certain currency against another.
Rollover	Generally, a term used to describe a short-term foreign exchange swap. The term is also used instead of "swap".
Settlement Date	See "Value Date"
Short Dates	Generally, transactions with value dates less than a month and, most commonly, less than a week.
Spot Date	The value date for a normal foreign exchange transaction concluded today where delivery of currencies usually occurs in two business days for most currencies, one business day for the Canadian dollar.

Term	Definition
Spot/Week	A type of short dated swap where the first date is spot and the second date is one week from spot.
Spread	The difference between the buying and selling rate for a given currency, or between the borrowing and lending rates in deposits.
Straddle	A long straddle is a combination of a long call and a put at the same strike price.
Straight Dates	Conventionally quoted forward dates based on the spot date. For example, one week, one month, two months, three months, six months, or one year (see "Odd Dates").
Strangle	The strangle is a combination of a long put and call with a different strike price.
Strike	The fixed price at which the owner of the option can purchase the underlying asset.
Swap	A simultaneous purchase and sale (or sale and purchase) of one currency against another for two different value dates.
Term	Details of a contract or life of contract.
Theta	Theta measures the sensitivity of the value of the option to the elapse of time. It is also known as time decay.
Time Value	The value of money taking into account the amount of interest earned, or inflation accrued, over a given amount of time.

Term	Definition
Tomorrow / Next	A type of short date swap transaction where the first date of the swap is tomorrow (the next business day) and the second date of the swap is the business day following that first date.
Value Date	The date on which a foreign exchange transaction is settled by the exchange of two currencies.
Vega	Measures the sensitivity to volatility with respect to the volatility of the underlying asset.
Volatility	A measure of the risk in a financial instrument for the variation of a price of a financial instrument over time.
Writer	The seller of an option contract who accepts a premium upfront in trade for taking the risk of a contract being exercised by the buyer during the period of the contract.

ISO Codes

Asia/Oceania

Currency Name	Currency	Geography
Bangladeshi Taka	BDT*	Asia/Oceania
Brunei Dollar	BND	Asia/Oceania
Chinese Yuan (Off-Shore Renminbi)	CNH	Asia/Oceania
Chinese Yuan (Renminbi)	CNY	Asia/Oceania
Fijian Dollar	FJD	Asia/Oceania
Indonesian Rupiah	IDR	Asia/Oceania
Indian Rupee	INR*	Asia/Oceania
Cambodian Riel	KHR	Asia/Oceania
South Korean Won	KRW*	Asia/Oceania
Laos Kip	LAK	Asia/Oceania
Sri Lankan Rupee	LKR	Asia/Oceania
Mongolian Tugrik	MNT	Asia/Oceania
Malaysian Ringgit	MYR*	Asia/Oceania
Nepalese Rupee	NPR	Asia/Oceania
Papua New Guinean Kina	PGK	Asia/Oceania
Philippine Peso	PHP	Asia/Oceania
Solomon Islands Dollar	SBD	Asia/Oceania
Singaporean Dollar	SGD	Asia/Oceania
Thai Baht	THB	Asia/Oceania
Tonga Pa'anga	TOP	Asia/Oceania
Taiwan Dollar	TWD*	Asia/Oceania
Vietnamese Dong	VND*	Asia/Oceania
Vanuatu Vatu	VUV	Asia/Oceania
Samoan Tala	WST	Asia/Oceania
Tahitian Franc	XPF	Asia/Oceania

Central/Eastern Europe

Currency Name	Currency	Geography
Albanian Lek	ALL	Central/Eastern Europe
Azerbaijan New Manat	AZN	Central/Eastern Europe
Bosnia Herzegovina Marka	BAM	Central/Eastern Europe
Bulgarian Lev	BGN	Central/Eastern Europe
Belarusian Ruble	BYR*	Central/Eastern Europe
Czech Koruna	CZK	Central/Eastern Europe
Croatian Kuna	HRK	Central/Eastern Europe
Hungarian Forint	HUF	Central/Eastern Europe
Icelandic Krona	ISK*	Central/Eastern Europe
Lithuanian Litas	LTL	Central/Eastern Europe
Latvian Lats	LVL	Central/Eastern Europe
Macedonian Denar	MKD	Central/Eastern Europe
Polish Zloty	PLN	Central/Eastern Europe
Romanian Leu	RON	Central/Eastern Europe
Serbian Dinar	RSD	Central/Eastern Europe
Russian Ruble	RUB*	Central/Eastern Europe

LatAm & Carribbean

Currency Name	Currency	Geography
Netherlands Antillean Guilder	ANG	LatAm & Carribbean
Argentine Peso	ARS**	LatAm & Carribbean
Barbadian Dollar	BBD	LatAm & Carribbean
Bermudian Dollar	BMD	LatAm & Carribbean
Bolivian Boliviano	BOB	LatAm & Carribbean
Brazilian Real	BRL**	LatAm & Carribbean
Bahamian Dollar	BSD	LatAm & Carribbean
Belize Dollar	BZD	LatAm & Carribbean
Chilean Peso	CLP**	LatAm & Carribbean
Colombian Peso	COP**	LatAm & Carribbean
Costa Rican Colon	CRC*	LatAm & Carribbean
Dominican Peso	DOP*	LatAm & Carribbean
Guatemalan Quetzal	GTQ	LatAm & Carribbean
Guyanese Dollar	GYD	LatAm & Carribbean
Honduran Lempira	HNL	LatAm & Carribbean
Haitian Gourde	HTG	LatAm & Carribbean
Jamaican Dollar	JMD	LatAm & Carribbean
Cayman Island Dollar	KYD	LatAm & Carribbean
Nicaraguan Cordoba	NIO	LatAm & Carribbean
Peruvian Nuevo Sol	PEN	LatAm & Carribbean
Paraguayan Guarani	PYG	LatAm & Carribbean
Surinamese Dollar	SRD	LatAm & Carribbean
Trinidad & Tobago Dollar	TTD	LatAm & Carribbean
Uruguayan Peso	UYU	LatAm & Carribbean
Venezuelan Bolivar Fuerte	VEF**	LatAm & Carribbean
East Caribbean Dollar	XCD*	LatAm & Carribbean

Majors

Currency Name	Currency	Geography
Australian Dollar	AUD	Majors
Canadian Dollar	CAD	Majors
Swiss Franc	CHF	Majors
Danish Krone	DKK	Majors
Euro	EUR	Majors
British Pound	GBP	Majors
Hong Kong Dollar	HKD	Majors
Japanese Yen	JPY	Majors
Mexican Peso	MXN	Majors
Norwegian Krone	NOK	Majors
New Zealand Dollar	NZD	Majors
Swedish Krona	SEK	Majors
Turkish New Lira	TRY	Majors
United States Dollar	USD	Majors
South African Rand	ZAR	Majors

Middle East/Africa

Currency Name	Currency	Geography
United Arab Emirates Dirham	AED	Middle East/Africa
Armenian Dram	AMD	Middle East/Africa
Angolan Kwanza	AOA	Middle East/Africa
Bahraini Dinar	BHD	Middle East/Africa
Burundian Franc	BIF	Middle East/Africa
Botswana Pula	BWP	Middle East/Africa
Congolese Franc	CDF	Middle East/Africa
Algerian Dinar	DZD	Middle East/Africa
Egyptian Pound	EGP	Middle East/Africa
Ethiopian Birr	ETB*	Middle East/Africa

Middle East/Africa (Cont.)

Currency Name	Currency	Geography
Georgian Lari	GEL	Middle East/Africa
Ghanaian Cedi	GHS	Middle East/Africa
Gambian Dalasi	GMD	Middle East/Africa
Guinean Franc	GNF	Middle East/Africa
Israeli New Shekel	ILS	Middle East/Africa
Jordanian Dinar	JOD	Middle East/Africa
Kenyan Shilling	KES	Middle East/Africa
Kuwaiti Dinar	KWD	Middle East/Africa
Kazakhstani Tenge	KZT	Middle East/Africa
Lebanese Pound	LBP	Middle East/Africa
Liberian Dollar	LRD	Middle East/Africa
Lesotho Loti	LSL	Middle East/Africa
Moroccan Dirham	MAD	Middle East/Africa
Malagsy Ariary	MGA	Middle East/Africa
Mauritanian Ouguiya	MRO	Middle East/Africa
Mauritian Rupee	MUR	Middle East/Africa
Malawian Kwacha	MWK	Middle East/Africa
Mozambican Metical	MZN*	Middle East/Africa
Namibian Dollar	NAD	Middle East/Africa
Nigerian Naira	NGN	Middle East/Africa
Omani Rial	OMR	Middle East/Africa
Pakistani Rupee	PKR*	Middle East/Africa
Qatari Rial	QAR	Middle East/Africa
Rwandan Franc	RWF	Middle East/Africa
Saudi Riyal	SAR	Middle East/Africa
Seychelles Rupee	SCR	Middle East/Africa
Sierra Leonean Leone	SLL	Middle East/Africa
Swaziland Lilangeni	SZL	Middle East/Africa

Middle East/Africa (Cont.)

Currency Name	Currency	Geography
Tunisian Dinar	TND	Middle East/Africa
Tanzanian Shilling	TZS	Middle East/Africa
Ugandan Shilling	UGX	Middle East/Africa
Central African States CFA Franc BEAC	XAF*	Middle East/Africa
Central African States CFA Franc BCEAO	XOF*	Middle East/Africa
Zambian Kwacha	ZMK	Middle East/Africa